Contents

Editorial Office 12501 Old Columbia Pike, Silver Spring, MD 20904
Come visit us at our Web sites: www.sabbathschoolpersonalministries.org
www.InStepWithJesus.org
Copyright © 2012 General Conference of Seventh-day Adventists

Author
Jane Thayer, PhD

Illustrator
Lars Justinen

Editor
Gary B. Swanson

Designer
Bruce Fenner

Sabbath
School
Personal
Ministries

In Step With Jesus is a series of four Bible study guides for new members of the Seventh-day Adventist family. It is prepared by the Sabbath School and Personal Ministries Department, published by the General Conference of Seventh-day Adventists, and printed by the Pacific Press® Publishing Association.

SEVENTH-DAY ADVENTIST
New Members' Bible Study Guide

IN STEP WITH JESUS

*T*our guides in Israel, Jordan, and Syria are kept busy year-round by Christians arriving from all over the world to follow in the footsteps of Jesus, to see the places where He healed people or taught them, and to imagine what it must have been like to be in the presence of the Son of God. But as the song, "I Walked Today Where Jesus Walked," says, we can walk where Jesus walked by living the life He lived. This quarter's lessons focus on how to begin this journey of a lifetime.

The lessons were specifically designed for those who are studying with Adventist friends or who have recently become members of the Seventh-day Adventist Church. The lessons will also be helpful to "renewed" members, those who have been away from the church for a while, or to current members who have recently gained a new longing to deepen their relationship with Jesus.

Beginning the journey with Jesus puts us on the path toward becoming like Him. On this path we encounter joy, healing, growth, and meaning in life. We will also be challenged by such troubles as temptation, sorrow, broken relationships, and sacrifice, for we are following the One who is described as "a Man of sorrows and acquainted with grief" (Isa. 53:3, NKJV). His death on the cross was the ultimate sacrifice. As His disciples we, too, can expect a bittersweet journey. This New Members' Bible Study Guide will serve as a counselor along the way.

Lessons 1 and 2 look at the decision to follow Jesus. Lessons 3 and 4 explore who Jesus is. Lessons 5, 6, and 7 confront some of the issues that face new believers as they make life changes. Lesson 8 assures disciples that Jesus is patient with them. Lessons 9, 10, 11, and 12 deal with the Bible: how Jesus used it, the authority of the Bible, and how to study it. Lesson 13 concludes with guidance for developing a devotional life.

Besides the basic question-and-answer format of studying the Bible, each lesson has additional features:

Walking With Jesus in the Real World, a personal story, will be found as part of Sunday's lesson. Although pseudonyms are typically used, all of the stories are from real experiences. As much as possible, each story relates to the topic of the lesson.

A Closer Look is a short piece that will focus on some biblical item that can use additional information or comment. Since space is limited, the focus will be brief.

Adventese is a short feature created to help new members understand the Adventist culture. It will define words that have special significance to Adventists. Occasionally, it also gives brief historical accounts of the Adventist Church and tells of current items of special interest.

Checking Up comes on Friday, after a week of study on a topic. This page continues the learning by using a quiz, a question, or activity to relate the lesson to the student's personal experience, and an activity to extend knowledge.

Consider This is a full-page column that is part of Friday's lesson. Usually, each week's "Consider This" piece will present nonbiblical information related to the week's topic. Information will come from the social sciences, history, etc.

A valuable feature for both students and teachers is an online Web site, which offers a variety of resources. Because it is online, it can be updated and added to at any time.

As you faithfully study each week's lessons, may you catch a vision of what it means to follow Jesus and may you find joy on the journey.

ANSWERING THE CALL OF JESUS

Key Texts: *Matthew 9:35–38; 28:19, 20; Mark 8:34, 35; John 1:35–51*

How did Jesus get His first disciples?
When Jesus invited someone to be His disciple, what was He offering them?
How did people respond to Jesus' invitation?
What does Jesus expect of His disciples?

This week's memory text: " 'Go therefore and make disciples of all the nations, baptizing them in the name of the Father and of the Son and of the Holy Spirit, teaching them to observe all things that I have commanded you; and lo, I am with you always, even to the end of the age' " (Matt. 28:19, 20, NKJV).

KEY TERMS

Call—In the Bible there are two kinds of call. The first is an invitation to be a disciple of Jesus, and it is given to everyone. The second is an invitation to serve God in a way that is unique to the individual receiving the call. This week's lesson deals with the first meaning of *call*.

Disciple—A disciple is one who has accepted Jesus' promise of eternal life and is becoming like Him as he or she lives in relationship with others.

What must it have been like to have Jesus look you in the face and say, "Follow Me"? This week's lesson will study people who had that experience, and we will see how they responded. As you study this lesson and live through this week, choose one of the following activities to do and be prepared to discuss your discoveries with your study group.

A. On Tuesday, we will learn what Jesus promised His disciples they would see as they followed Him. As you follow Jesus this week, make a mental note of what you are learning about Him and about yourself.

B. Ask two or three friends or family members if they have ever experienced Jesus calling them to follow Him. What method did Jesus use to call them and how did they respond?

Walking With Jesus in the Real World

Hearing Jesus' Call Through Friends

In February during the year Kelly was working on a master's degree at a state university, she was surfing the Internet when she decided it might be interesting to find a date for Valentine's Day. She looked through classified ads under "personals" and found an entry from a young man named Brian who mentioned the word *Christian* in his description. He had not posted a photograph, but Kelly contacted him anyway.

In a short time she invited him to attend a youth rally in a nearby city. Surrounded by several girlfriends, she drove to the city and met Brian at the youth rally. "He was better looking than I thought he would be," she said. The next day Brian, Kelly, and her girlfriends spent the day at an amusement park. By the end of the day, the consensus of the young women was that Brian was OK.

Fast-forward two years: Kelly and Brian were married.

Now they faced the adventure of blending two lives that had come from vastly different religious backgrounds, yet they were both looking for something honest and real. Kelly had grown up in a very strict home as a pastor's kid. From her earliest years, she was told that her behavior determined whether or not Jesus liked her. "To think that my behavior could influence Jesus' emotions gave me the need to be good and to try to make everyone happy. I had so much guilt." Even as a young adult, she had no assurance that Jesus accepted her. The only assurance she had was the admonition, "As long as you're worried about what God thinks of you, you are saved."

Even though Brian's parents had seen to it that he attended Sunday School, he grew up in a secular home where there was no evidence of a living faith. His mother constantly told him how much he disappointed her and hurt her. In his church youth group, he saw movies about the end times that scared him. He was forced into accepting God because of his fear of eternal punishment in hell. After graduating from college, he moved into his own apartment and for the next several years lived a lonely life. Although he had several casual friends, he had no one to talk with about serious matters. Long before this, he had quit Sunday School.

Not long after they were married, a Christian couple who lived nearby invited Brian and Kelly to a small group gathering every Friday night. For two years they met every week, reading and discussing books. Brian and Kelly began to see God in a different way. Through their friendship with caring Christians and through the books they read, Brian and Kelly heard Jesus call them to follow Him in a new, joyful way. Kelly says, "I began to realize that Jesus has the answer to any problem you have—including anxiety and guilt. He can heal and restore." And Brian says, "I began to follow Jesus because I wanted to, not because I feared eternal punishment."

Monday

CALLING THE FIRST DISCIPLES

During the time of Jesus' public ministry on earth, many people came to hear Him teach or to be healed by Him. In fact, one time the crowd was so great He had to get in a little fishing boat and push out into the water to get away from the press of the people so they could hear Him.

But twelve men had a special relationship with Jesus. These men were known as **the Twelve** or the disciples. They came from several different occupations and levels of society. We don't know the circumstances around the "calling" of all twelve of the disciples, but the Gospels do record the call of six of them.

The longest account of calling is in John 1:35–51. The location of this story is near the Jordan River where **John the Baptist** was baptizing people. So the person referred to as "John" in the first verse is John the Baptist. Read John 1:35–51. As you read, visualize the scenes as they occur.

The first two men in this story (Andrew and probably John, the author of this Gospel) began following Jesus even though He had not "called" them to follow Him. It appears that they were curious to learn about Jesus. What must have motivated their curiosity? Read verses 35–37.

Jesus invited these two disciples to the place where He was staying. How much time did they spend with Jesus? See verse 39.

• How do we know that Andrew was overjoyed with his experience of visiting with Jesus? Read verses 41, 42.

The next day Jesus invited Philip to be His disciple. What similar response did Philip make after spending time with Jesus? Read verse 45.

• In your opinion, why were Andrew and Philip so eager to tell someone else about Jesus?

Think about these questions: What has been your experience of getting acquainted with Jesus? Is it valuable enough to share?

KEY TERMS

The Twelve—New Testament writers sometimes refer to the 12 disciples of Jesus simply as "the Twelve." These 12 were later appointed by Jesus as apostles or leaders.

John the Baptist—This man was a cousin of Jesus and a prophet whose mission was to prepare people to recognize Jesus as the Messiah.

Tuesday
INVITATION AND PROMISE

One of Evelyn's seminary teachers assigned her class to read the same passage of Scripture every day for one week—and each day to write what new ideas they had learned from the text that day. Evelyn thought this was a rather pointless exercise—until the week was over. Then she began to understand that reading a text over and over, and pondering its meaning, truly does give deeper insight than a once-over reading. For this reason, read again John 1:35–51 and look for answers to these questions:

• What can you learn about the first two men called by Jesus to be His disciples? See vv. 35–42.

• Notice carefully the words that Jesus uses to call His disciples. Write only the words spoken by Jesus.

   v. 39

   v. 43

In Jesus' first discussions with the disciples, He uses the words, "You will see." These words serve as promises. What does Jesus promise those who follow Him? What is He going to show them?

   vv. 38, 39

   v. 50

   v. 51

A CLOSER LOOK

The word *gospel* has two important meanings.

One meaning is "good news" about Jesus and what He has done for us. That is the definition used in the expression, "gospel commission."

The second meaning is "a book in the New Testament that records the life and teachings of Jesus." The Bible is composed of 66 books written over 1,000 years. These books are of different literary forms. There are history books, law books, long letters, songs, gospels, and other forms.

A gospel is a special type of literary form that was designed for the specific purpose of announcing the "good news" of Jesus. There are four Gospels: Matthew, Mark, Luke, and John. All four appear at the beginning of the New Testament. Because the first three are similar in style and content, they are called the Synoptic Gospels. The fourth Gospel, the book of John, focuses on the divinity of Christ and has an evangelistic purpose. In this Gospel, Jesus talks a lot about Himself and much of this information is given only to His disciples.

Wednesday

WHO RESPONDED TO JESUS?

We know that twelve men, who are known as the Twelve or the twelve disciples, followed Jesus closely for three years. In addition, Jesus had other disciples. According to Luke 10:1, He trained a group of 70 or 72 disciples. A group of women disciples followed Him and helped in His ministry in various ways (Matt. 27:55).

Huge crowds also followed Him. These were not disciples, but it was Jesus' purpose to make disciples of them. In Matthew 9:35–38, read this description of Jesus and the crowds, in some Bible versions "multitudes." What was His concern for them?

Although many people did choose to follow Jesus, many others did not. Read about the invitation that Jesus gave to two men and record their responses.

- "Another person":
     Call (Luke 9:59)
     Response (v. 59)

- Rich young ruler:
     Call (Matt. 19:21)
     Response (v. 22)

- How similar or different are these responses from responses that people today make to Jesus' invitation?

Because the Jewish people had for generations been expecting a Messiah, a deliverer who would free them from Roman occupation and bring unheard-of prosperity, they were attracted to this man Jesus who healed people and who could feed thousands. Maybe He was the Messiah.

But sometimes His words puzzled them and caused them to turn away. What did He tell those who were considering whether to follow Him? Read Mark 8:34, 35.

A CLOSER LOOK

Lamb of God
    This title, given to Jesus by John the Baptist, refers to the sacrificial lamb that was offered as an atonement for sin.

Thursday
JESUS' TASK FOR HIS DISCIPLES

For three years Jesus was with the Twelve preparing them for the day when He would no longer be with them. These disciples learned from Jesus as they listened to His sermons and His stories. They observed His response to the crowds and His talks with individuals. They saw Him heal people, and they saw Him combat the hypocrisy of the religious leaders. After the crucifixion of Jesus and His resurrection and before He returned to heaven, Jesus revealed to the disciples His task for them. These instructions are found among the last words in the Gospel of Matthew. They are called the gospel commission. Read the gospel commission and identify the two words that are the heart of the task Jesus gave His disciples.

• Two key words (Matt. 28:19):

• To accomplish this task, what methods were they to use? (vv. 19, 20)

   The gospel commission is no small task. It includes the entire world population. It would be, in fact, an impossible task except for the two statements that introduce and conclude the command. One is an announcement; the other is a promise. What are these statements and how do they impact the "great task"?

• Announcement (v. 18):

• Promise (v. 20)

ADVENTESE*

Sabbath School Quarterly: This term is a shortened expression that refers to Bible study guides that are published in four issues each year and that are prepared by the General Conference. In fact, Sabbath School lessons have been published since 1852. *The Adult Bible Study Guide* is (obviously) for adults. *The Collegiate Quarterly,* or *CQ,* is for young adults of college age. Both of these 13-lesson quarterlies deal with the same topics. Wherever you go around the globe, Adventists will be studying the same Sabbath School lesson on the same Sabbath, printed in their own language. *The Adult Bible Study Guide* is translated into more than 80 languages. The "quarterly" you hold in your hand has been designed to serve the needs and interests of new believers.

---

* "Adventese" is an invented word that means words or expressions with unique meanings in the Adventist community of believers.

CHECKING UP

Circle the letter of the best answer to each of the following questions.

1. In what occupation were most of the 12 disciples working?
    A. Beggars
    B. Common laborers
    C. Priests
    D. Teachers

2. What was the typical wording of the invitation that Jesus gave to people He wanted as disciples?
    A. Be My disciple.
    B. Obey My commands.
    C. Follow Me.
    D. Go and sin no more.

3. How many disciples did Jesus have altogether?
    A. 12
    B. 70 or 72
    C. 12 plus 70 or 72
    D. More than listed in C

4. Which of the following actions is not one of the strategies that Jesus gave for making disciples?
    A. Teaching the Word
    B. Offering good health
    C. Baptizing
    D. Going everywhere

Examine Your Own Experience

Place a + before a statement that is true; place a 0 before a statement that is false. At the end of each statement, there will be directions asking you to tell more. This "tell more" may be done in your study group.

_____ 1. I recognize that it is Jesus calling me to be His disciple. Explain.

_____ 2. It took me a long time to respond to His invitation. Why?

_____ 3. I am learning almost every day something new about what it means to be a disciple of Jesus. Give an example.

More resources on this topic can be found at http://www.InStepWithJesus.org/Journey.

"Going" With the Gospel Commission

The Seventh-day Adventist Church was officially organized in the United States in 1863. Just eleven years later, in 1874, the church sent out its first missionary to a country outside of North America. John Nevins Andrews, theologian, evangelist, and intellectual, was sent to Europe where he helped found a publishing house in Switzerland and an Adventist periodical in the French language. His wife having died two years earlier, he left his home shores as a single parent with two children, Charles and Mary.

Thousands of others would follow in Andrews's footsteps to leave their home country compelled by the gospel commission of Matthew 28 to carry the "good news" of Jesus Christ to countries throughout the world.

Today the Adventist Church is currently active in more than 200 countries. It has churches, schools of every academic level, and hospitals and clinics to meet the spiritual, intellectual, and physical needs of people.

The "Go" command of the gospel commission is not limited to work outside of one's own country or even neighborhood or family. Sometimes the word is translated "as you go," meaning, as you go about your daily activities, you can give the good news of Jesus Christ. And if you also want to help in the worldwide mission of "going," there are ways to do so without leaving your own home. Consider Cheryl Erickson of North Dakota and her 1.5-acre backyard pumpkin patch.

Cheryl began growing pumpkins when the region's farm economy withered. "I started looking into specialty crops that would be productive in a very small space," she says. After considering dried flowers, herbs, and lavender, she settled on pumpkins. In the first eight years of her new project, her pumpkin money built 11 churches in India. Each cost between $3,000 and $7,000. Her pumpkins sell for $2 each.

Cheryl and her husband, Dwight, plant, cultivate, water, pray over, harvest, haul, wash, load, unload, and sell an average of 120 tons of pumpkins during a typical harvest. The couple receives help from their four children and a slew of neighbors, friends, and church volunteers ranging from age 4 to 89.

For more current stories of missions, go to http://www.adventistmission.org.

2

THE JOURNEY BEGINS

Now that I have decided to follow Jesus, where do I begin?
Are the reasons for following Jesus stronger than the temptations not to follow Him?
Why do so many people give up on Jesus?
Am I worthy to be a disciple?

> **This week's memory text:** *" 'If anyone desires to come after Me, let him deny himself, and take up his cross daily, and follow Me. For whoever desires to save his life will lose it, but whoever loses his life for My sake will save it' "* (Luke 9:23, 24, NKJV).

Sunday

Because you have chosen to accept Jesus' offer of a more abundant life, you have begun a journey that will last your entire lifetime. The concept of "journey" to discipleship is central. A journey is not a single event. It requires time and progress, a destination.

This week's study will ask questions about your own experience of beginning the journey and will look at how disciples followed Jesus when He was on earth. It will consider what Jesus expected of His disciples. The memory text for this week is a good place to start. Why would anyone be willing to lose his or her life for Jesus?

Walking With Jesus in the Real World

Growing With Others in a Small Group

Feeling dissatisfied with her relationship with God, Georgina asked an associate pastor, "How can I become more mature in my Christian life?" The pastor suggested a book for her to read and later invited her to join a small group that she—the pastor—was starting. This Georgina did.

The group of about 12 people of various ages meets each week during the Sabbath School hour. Although the group has been going for only four months, it has already made a difference in Georgina's life. "I really feel connected, like I have a family," she says. "All of us feel free to talk about what is going on in our lives. And I feel a sense of accountability to study, to attend each week, and to support my new friends in prayer."

And support them in prayer, she does. During a discussion about the life of Jesus, the question came up, "How could Jesus have lived a perfect life?"

Someone in the group said, "For one thing, He spent a lot of time in prayer. Sometimes He even spent the whole night in prayer."

That comment made Georgina think about her own prayer life. Even though she has a managerial position at a large corporation and works 40-plus hours a week, it was already her practice to rise early enough to spend time in prayer and Bible study before going to work. But thinking about the prayer life of Jesus and the depth of His communion with the Father, she decided that her morning time with God did not give her enough time for prayer. So, she reset her alarm clock somewhat earlier and now spends significant time in prayer, in memorizing Scripture, and in studying her Bible.

"It is wonderful to have this deposit of Scripture in my mind," Georgina says. And how does she spend her time in prayer each morning? "I pray for the concerns of everyone in our small group; I pray for all of my family members; my boss and coworkers; and for myself," she says.

It was her small group that provided Georgina with the inspiration and motivation to strengthen her relationship with God. Deepening relationships with other believers in the small group setting seems to also deepen our relationship with God.

BEGINNING THE JOURNEY

To be a disciple of Jesus and follow Him means more than to believe certain things. How has your life changed since you began to follow Jesus? Can you picture yourself among those people who literally followed Jesus? He took fishermen, a tax collector, and other laborers and gave them a life they never could have imagined. Read Luke 8:1–15 carefully and try to visualize how Jesus taught His disciples.

Where was the learning occurring?

It is sometimes thought that Jesus had only 12 disciples. It is true that He chose 12 men to be His closest companions and to receive His in-depth teaching and training and to be leaders after He left earth, but others were also considered disciples. Who besides the Twelve followed Him on this occasion?

In this passage Jesus teaches through a **parable**. What does the parable tell us about people who begin the journey with Jesus?

• To whom did Jesus tell this parable?

• To whom did Jesus interpret the parable?

Why did Jesus have different ways of teaching different groups of people? In Mark 10:32, note carefully the details in this text that give another glimpse of Jesus' teaching. Where were Jesus and His disciples?

• If you were an artist painting this scene, where would you place Jesus and where would you place the disciples?

• What does Mark 10:32 tell you about being a disciple?

• Summarize what you learned in this single text about how Jesus taught the disciples?

• Are these same methods of learning from Jesus available to you? Explain.

KEY TERMS

Parable—A short story that illustrates a religious or ethical point. This was a favorite teaching strategy of Jesus.

WHY HIM?

Jesus declared that He had come to give people life, even a more abundant life (John 10:9, 10). Eugene Peterson writes joyfully that Jesus brings us "life, life, and more life." Speaking to those who wanted to follow Him, Jesus redefined "life" in a startling way. Read Luke 9:23, 24. How can this **paradox** be explained?

If following Jesus means making changes in life—even uncomfortable changes—why is He so compelling that a person is willing to begin this journey? When He was on earth and people could see and hear Him, what attracted them to Him and made them willing to leave all to follow Him?

Read Matthew 4:23–25 and Mark 1:35–39. Imagine what you would have thought about Jesus if you had been there. What did the people see?

Imagine the challenges of being God in human form. How could Jesus reveal to people His true identity? The miracle He performed provided important clues. When the disciple John wrote a record of Jesus' life, he gave the **miracles** a name that gives a clue to their purpose. Find that name as you read about another miracle in John 6:1–15. What is this name?

• What did the miracles accomplish? Read John 2:11, 23; 3:2; 6:2; 7:3.

Something else made Jesus differ from all other **rabbis** the people had seen. At the end of the long Sermon on the Mount (Matthew 5–7), how did the people respond and why? Read Matthew 7:28, 29.

When the chief priests and the Pharisees became concerned over Jesus' popularity, they sent temple guards to arrest Him, but the guards returned empty-handed. According to John 7:45, 46, what was their reason?

If you have ever been concerned or confused about some issue or question for years and then hear someone explain the matter, don't the words bring relief and joy? As you are learning more each day about Jesus, have you had such "aha" moments of understanding?

• If someone were to ask you what attracted you to Jesus, what would you tell them?

KEY TERMS

Paradox—A statement that is seemingly contradictory yet true.
Miracle—A supernatural intervention in human affairs that cannot be explained by known natural laws.
Rabbi—Someone qualified through careful study to explain Jewish law; a title of respect.

WHY DOESN'T EVERYONE FOLLOW JESUS?

Some 2,000 years after Jesus was on earth, the evidence keeps mounting that He changed the world. His Word and His Spirit still speak with authority and power. Millions follow Him as their Savior. Yet, in some parts of the world, few believe in Him. And even in countries that were one time nominally Christian, many people who once followed Him have turned away.

Why? You can probably list several reasons that people give for not believing in or following Jesus. But Jesus could see through the transparency of people's excuses, and He explained to His disciples the underlying reasons. Do you think these reasons still exist? Let's look at a few.

After Jesus told the parable of the sower (Luke 8:11–15), He explained plainly to His disciples that the parable portrayed different ways that people respond to the Word of God. Identify the reasons Jesus listed.

1.
2.
3.

In His private discussion with Nicodemus (John 3:18–21), Jesus explained why people don't believe in Him. What reason was given?

When the temple officers returned without arresting Jesus (Tuesday's lesson), the Pharisees challenged them with two rhetorical questions and a comment. What were they implying? Read John 7:47–49.

• Which of these excuses that people make for not following Jesus still exist today?

ADVENTESE

The Seventh-day Adventist Church is organized with a representative form of church government. The levels of church structure lead from the individual believer to the worldwide church organization:
- **Local church:** Individual members.
- **Conference or Mission:** Churches in a state, province, or territory.
- **Union Conference:** Conferences in a geographic area, often a grouping of states or a whole country.
- **Division:** One of 13 areas into which the entire world has been organized. The North American Division (NAD) includes the United States, Canada, and Bermuda.
- **General Conference (GC):** Represents the entire world church. Its headquarters are in Silver Spring, Maryland, U.S.A.

Thursday
WILL I BE A HYPOCRITE?

People often say they don't want to claim to be a Christian or to join a Christian church because they don't want to be a **hypocrite**, like all the other Christians. It is possible to be called a Christian and be a member of a church for years and yet fail to be growing more and more like Jesus. People can exhibit attitudes and behaviors that show they are not "dying daily" to self or treating others as Jesus would. If you haven't already met some, you will.

Not only can you see that some people are not living up to the name of Christian, but you also know that you are dealing with your own sins. You may even agonize over the question, "If I'm a sinner who keeps sinning, what right do I have to call myself a Christian?" In Mark 2:15–17, Jesus spoke to this issue when some Pharisees were condemning Him for associating with people their culture classified as sinners. How did Jesus answer their criticism?

People themselves chose whether to follow Jesus or not. There was not a single instance in which Jesus turned someone away from following Him simply because that person was a sinner. Even though Jesus knew beforehand that His own disciple Judas was going to betray Him, what indication is there that Jesus offered him acceptance and trust? Read John 12:4–6.

Jesus told a parable once that helps to explain why it is not the role of a church to try to "weed out" all of the sinners. What would be an unintended consequence? Read Matthew 13:24–30.

Christians are not hypocrites because they are sinners; Christians are hypocrites only if they pretend that they are not sinners or fail to allow Jesus to transform us.

A CLOSER LOOK

Discipleship As a Journey

Careful readers of the Gospels soon notice that there are many phrases and place names that picture Jesus and His disciples as traveling across the countryside and through towns and villages.

One New Testament scholar concludes that all the references to travel emphasize "the fact that discipleship is active and not passive, that it means leaving one's own way to follow Jesus on his way."*

KEY TERMS

Hypocrite—Someone who pretends to have virtues or qualities that he or she does not truly have.

---

*Dennis Sweetland, *Mark: From Death to Life* (Hyde Park, N.Y.: New City Press, 2000), p. 52.

Friday

CHECKING UP

Circle all of the responses that are correct.

1. What did people see and hear that first attracted them to Jesus?
   A. He was a rabbi.
   B. He taught with authority.
   C. He performed miracles.
   D. He always fed them.

2. How did Jesus' teaching of His disciples differ from how He taught others?
   A. He did not use parables to teach His disciples, but used parables to teach the crowds.
   B. He sometimes took His disciples aside and explained the meaning of the parables, but He did not explain the parables to the crowd.
   C. He took His disciples with Him on His travels; the crowd just showed up when Jesus was in their area.

Extend Your Learning

3. This lesson could not list all of the reasons that people gave for not following Jesus. Can you locate any other reasons that are mentioned in Scripture? Include the texts.

4. Can you think of any reason that people today give for not following Jesus that differs from the reasons recorded in the Gospels? If so, what?

Examine Your Own Experience

What first attracted you to Jesus?

Do you think that if you follow Jesus each day that you will have the same character at the end of a year or five years that you have today?

Read "The Power of the Small Group" on the next page. What are your thoughts about participating in a small group?

More resources on this topic can be found at http://www.InStepWithJesus.org/Journey.

The Power of the Small Group

Steven Garber, who has taught college students in a number of settings, noticed a puzzling pattern. Young adults, who had attended Christian colleges and seemed to understand the relationship between their beliefs and their way of life, would—once they entered the secular world—"slowly, inch by inch, . . . disconnect what they said they believed from how they lived."* Others, however, remained faithful to beliefs and lifestyle.

Because he wanted to find out what made the difference between faithfulness and abandonment, he interviewed about two dozen people who still remained faithful to Christ 20 years after college graduation. He found that they all had three characteristics in common: (1) While in their Christian college, some Christian—usually a teacher—mentored them; (2) while in college they had gained a Christian worldview that was strong enough to withstand secularism; and (3) after leaving college, they had found a group of like-minded Christians with whom they shared life and common values. Having had a positive college experience was not enough. They had to *continue* to be with others who were following Christ.

In today's way of life, community seldom happens naturally. Over a lifetime, people move many times, uprooting themselves from their extended family, their friends, and their faith community. Loneliness is a common complaint; beliefs and the Christian way of life are weakened. The journey of discipleship, as Jesus demonstrated, is best taken with a small group of people. In today's culture, local congregations have found that the "small group" is a powerful strategy for creating community among people who want to join the journey of discipleship with Jesus.

If you are not already a member of a small group, discuss with your pastor or teacher how to find or initiate a small group where you can experience a supporting community.

KEY TERMS

Small group—A group of 6 to 12 people who provide a discipling community, meeting regularly in an informal setting. It offers these elements: unconditional acceptance, confidentiality, Bible study, prayer, accountability, and ministry.

---

* Steven Garber, *Fabric of Faithfulness: Weaving Together Belief and Behavior* (Wheaton, Ill.: InterVarsity Press, 1996), p. 33.

LESSON

WHO IS JESUS?

Key Texts: *Deuteronomy 18:15; Matthew 14:22–33; 17:5; Luke 1:26–33; 2:25–35; 23:35–39; John 1:40–42; 6:1–15; Acts 9:1–9; 22:1–11*

Do I really know who Jesus is?
What can eyewitnesses to His life tell me?
How does my understanding of who Jesus is affect the way I live?

This week's memory text: *"While he was still speaking, a bright cloud enveloped them, and a voice from the cloud said, 'This is my Son, whom I love; with him I am well pleased. Listen to him!' "* (Matt. 17:5, NIV).

The role of eyewitnesses is to testify to what they have seen and heard; in other words to establish the facts. Luke said that he wrote his Gospel to give an account of things "just as those who from the beginning were eyewitnesses . . . delivered them to us" (Luke 1:2, NKJV).

One of those eyewitnesses, John, began one of his books with his personal testimony that he was recording that "which we have seen with our eyes, which we have looked upon, and our hands have handled, concerning the Word of life" (1 John 1:1, NKJV). This week we will study eyewitness accounts of those who knew Jesus when He walked this earth and consider the titles by which they identified Him.

Walking With Jesus in the Real World
Saved by an Accident

The accident happened in a split second. The driver had been drinking and so had Diane, who was sitting in the back seat. At age 21, the accident left Diane so injured that it was thought she would never walk again. During her recovery, she had a stroke. She couldn't remember her mother's phone number. She couldn't tell time. In addition to physical therapy, the doctors ordered speech and occupational therapy.

When she was released from the hospital, still in a wheelchair, she discovered that all her friends had "disappeared." She was lonely and had a lot of time to think. Before the accident, she'd been very popular and did a lot of drinking with her friends. She was very good at basketball. Yet, she says, things hadn't seemed right. Something had seemed to be missing in life.

In her childhood home, the name of Jesus was never mentioned. Neither she nor her parents attended church of any kind. Her only knowledge of God and Jesus came from what she picked up from living in a post-Christian culture. She knew enough about Jesus to be angry with Him. She was angry because He didn't have enough power to prevent terrible things from happening. The devil seemed to have more power. Even though she heard glorious things about Jesus, she thought she could live life better her own way.

The accident shocked Diane into realizing that she had to change her life. This reminded her of Kevin, a young man she had once dated. He was the only person from her past who had any connection to Christianity. She called him, but he was reluctant to talk to her because their relationship had ended unpleasantly. Finally, however, he agreed to come see her.

"Why did God let this happen to me?" Diane asked.

Kevin's answer was rather blunt. He told her that the accident had not happened because of God but because of her own choices.

Kevin and Diane began to date again. One day when they were together, she said to him, "I want to go to church." Kevin, who had grown up an Adventist but had not attended church for a long time, looked around for an Adventist church and took her there.

Six months later, after Bible studies, Diane was baptized. And Kevin, who had been out of the church, was also later re-baptized. "I was a blessing to him," Diane says, "while he was being a blessing to me." Sometime later they were married.

Diane's understanding of Jesus has changed. "Now I know that Jesus has the power of God. He came from heaven to be human." Her favorite parable of Jesus is that in which a mustard seed grows from being the smallest of seeds to being a great plant. She says she is like the mustard seed. "I came from not knowing Jesus to learning this wonderful news about Him. I want to tell as many people as I can so that they can have this great experience with Him that I have."

Monday

THE THIRTEENTH DISCIPLE

Did you know that the Bible includes an account of Jesus calling a thirteenth disciple? This calling produced history's most famous conversion story. What makes it so meaningful to us today is that Jesus called this disciple *after* He had ascended to heaven. In other words, just as He called this disciple, He can call people today. There are two accounts of this incident, one recorded by Luke, the author of the Acts of the Apostles, and one recorded by the person who was called. Read the account recorded by Luke in Acts 9:1–9. Where was the person when Jesus called him and what was he doing?

• How did this encounter with the risen Jesus physically affect him?

• What important question did Saul ask Jesus?

    Saul changed his name to Paul and, after some study, he was accepted into the Christian community. He risked his life many times traveling, preaching, and teaching about Jesus. Several years later after his conversion on the road to Damascus, he returned to Jerusalem. Soon the whole city became enraged over this man whom the religious leaders thought was subverting their laws, so they arrested him. Paul was allowed to address the crowd, and he began his speech establishing his "Jewishness" and telling the story of his conversion. Read his personal testimony in Acts 22:1–11.

• What two questions does Paul say that he asked Jesus?

    1.

    2.

    These are the very same two questions that every disciple (that means us) must ask—not just once, but throughout our lifetime. And the answers will continue to change us as we become more faithful in our following of Jesus. This week's lesson and next week's lesson will focus on the first question. The second question will be dealt with in all the following lessons as we continue to learn more about Jesus and His guidance for us.

Tuesday

WHO IS JESUS? THE MESSIAH?

Few of us realize the influence that our own culture has on us. Common experiences give a family or a city or even a country common expectations, fears, joys, and unique words to express those feelings. For example, people in the United States have emotional attachments to such terms as "Fourth of July," "9/11," "Inauguration Day," "West Coast," "Bible belt," and many more. Every country has its own insider words. In the time of Jesus, one of the most important words that held an entire people's hopes and dreams was "**Messiah**."

When Joseph and Mary took the Baby Jesus to Jerusalem to bless Him, a common practice of that culture, the priest Simeon said that God's promise to him had been fulfilled. What was that promise? Read Luke 2:25–35.

Right after Andrew met Jesus, he went looking for his brother Peter to tell him about Jesus. Whom did he say he had found? See John 1:40–42.

After the twelve disciples had been with Jesus for a while and had witnessed some of His miracles and heard His teachings, Jesus asked them, "Who do people say I am?" Read Mark 8:27–30. Whom did the people think Jesus might be?

• Whom did Peter say Jesus was?

When Jesus was on the cross, what titles did the rulers—and even one of the thieves—question? Read Luke 23:35–39.

From Jesus' infancy to His death, the title Messiah was associated with Him. For some it was a title of hope; for others, a title of contempt fueled by doubt.

KEY TERMS

Messiah/Christ—Both words mean "the **anoint**ed one." *Messiah* is the Hebrew word used in the Old Testament; *Christ* is the Greek word used in the New Testament. See "A Closer Look" on page 25.

Anoint—To smear or rub or pour oil on. This was a sacred rite of consecration for kings, priests, and prophets.

WHO IS JESUS? A PROPHET?

No special word from the Lord had come to the people of Israel for more than 400 years, since the words of the last Old Testament prophet **Malachi** had been written. But because of two promises in Scripture, the people were looking and longing for a great **prophet** to appear. Who spoke the promises and what kind of prophet did each speaker say would come?

Deuteronomy 18:15.
    Speaker
    Type of prophet to come
Malachi 4:5, 6.
    Speaker
    Type of prophet to come

With everyone expecting a great prophet to appear, imagine what the people thought when John the Baptist began preaching and attracting great crowds? Read John 1:19–23.

• Whom did they think John might be?
• What was John's reply?
• How did he identify himself?

When Jesus began healing people and serving them in other miraculous ways, people began to wonder if He was "the prophet" who had been predicted. Read the story of such a miracle and note the people's reaction in John 6:1–15.

• What was the miracle?
• What was the response of the people?

The thought of having a great prophet who could perform miracles for them excited the people so much that they wanted to make Jesus king. But Moses had not instructed them to make this new prophet a king. What had he told the people to do regarding the prophet? Read Deuteronomy 18:15.

Since Christians believe that Jesus is that great Prophet, do you think Moses' instruction is an appropriate way to relate to Jesus?

KEY TERMS

Malachi—This last of the so-called minor prophets of the Old Testament tells us nothing about himself. It is thought that this book was written about a century after the return of the Jews from Babylonian captivity.

Prophet—A person called and qualified by God to be His spokesperson to His people. Religious instruction is the primary duty of a prophet. In Old Testament times the great prophets were Moses and Elijah.

Deuteronomy—The fifth book of the Old Testament. It contains Moses' three great and final speeches in which he reviews the experiences and lessons of the Exodus.

Thursday
WHO IS JESUS? SON OF GOD?

No other title makes such dramatic and bold claims for Jesus as the title "Son of God." Though it is true that those who love God and serve Him are often referred to as the sons and daughters of God, when the title is given to Jesus, its meaning includes divine power, authority, mission, and equality. Anyone today making that claim would be under the care of a psychiatrist. Yet people and angels gave that title to Jesus from before His birth to His death.

• Who was the first to call Jesus the Son of the Most High? Read Luke 1:26–33.

• On what occasion?

At the opening of Jesus' public ministry, who was the first to assign the title Son of God to Him? Read John 1:32.

On two occasions God Himself, being described as the Voice from heaven or the Voice from a cloud, refers to Jesus as His Son. What are these two occasions?

• Matthew 3:3–17
• Matthew 17:1–8

Satan used the term "Son of God" when he tempted Jesus in the wilderness. Read Matthew 4:3, 6. How and why was Satan using the term?

• What miracle caused the disciples to call Jesus the Son of God? Read Matthew 14:22–33.

As Jesus was dying on the cross, passersby, priests, and teachers referred to the title "Son of God." And immediately after His death, the centurion and other guards also used that title. With what tone did the passersby and leaders use the title? Read Matthew 27:39–44.

• What tone did the centurion use? Read verses 50–54.

The crowd and the centurion witnessed the same events. What do you think made the difference in their reaction?

A CLOSER LOOK

Israel

"Sometime during the 2nd or 3rd century B.C. in response to oppression by the Greeks and the Romans, the hope developed that God would send a deliverer to His people. Three texts in particular generated this hope: Genesis 49:10 (the scepter shall not depart from Judah); Numbers 24:17 (a scepter shall rise out of Israel); Isaiah 11:1–6 (There shall come forth a Rod from the stem of Jesse). Many different interpretations were given to these rather cryptic texts. However, all of Jewish literature agreed on this one point: 'He will be a political ruler and national hero . . . [and] deliver Israel from its oppressors and restore the authority of the law.' "*

---

* Geoffrey Bromiley, ed., *The International Bible Encyclopedia* (Grand Rapids, Mich.: Eerdmans, 1979), CD-ROM.

25

Friday

CHECKING UP

Circle the correct title.

1. Which title given by others to Jesus was based on their remembrance of Moses and Elijah?
   A. Messiah
   B. Prophet
   C. Son of God

2. Which title was used by the angel Gabriel, by God, and by Satan when talking to or about Jesus?
   A. Messiah
   B. Prophet
   C. Son of God

3. Which title given by others to Jesus grew out of their desire for deliverance from Roman rule?
   A. Messiah
   B. Prophet
   C. Son of God

Extend Your Learning

Look up additional titles that other people gave to Jesus.
   Matthew 1:23
   Luke 2:11
   John 1:29
   Acts 3:15

Examine Your Own Experience

What implications does Jesus' title of Son of God have for the way you personally relate to Him? Let's revisit two texts and look at a new one. In each text, what action is linked with the title Son of God? Give your answer in just one or two words.
   Matthew 14:33
   Matthew 17:5
   John 15:9, 10

What commitment will you make to improve, by the grace of God, one or more of the above behaviors?

More resources on this topic can be found at http://www.InStepWithJesus.org/Journey.

Whom Do People Today Think Jesus Is?

What does popular culture say about Jesus? Popular culture comes to us through the mass media: television, movies, radio, the Internet, books, magazines, and newspapers. These media do not present one picture of Jesus. Sometimes the people behind the media do their best to portray the Jesus of the Bible. At other times, it seems that they invent fanciful stories that appeal to skeptical people or create controversy in order to sell their product.

The media have portrayed Jesus as a superstar, as a talk-show host, a hippie, a rock star, a police officer, the husband of Mary Magdalene. Even when these portrayals are meant to teach something good, they blur the distinction between fact and fiction. People who do not know what the Bible teaches about Jesus have no standard by which to evaluate the accuracy of these media statements and portrayals of Jesus. Their ideas of Jesus become fuzzy, and, if they are casual Christians, their faith wavers.

Survey polls taken in North America consistently show that a large percent of people believe that Jesus is the Son of God. These same people, however, may not understand the implications of that belief—at least they do not live the implications.

It is common for people who do not believe in God or who are followers of some religion other than Christianity to say that they respect Jesus as a great moral teacher. In his book *Mere Christianity,* C. S. Lewis pointed out the fallacy of this position:

"I am trying here to prevent anyone from saying the really foolish thing that people often say about Him: 'I'm ready to accept Jesus as a great moral teacher, but I don't accept His claim to be God.' That is the one thing we must not say. A man who was merely a man and said the sort of things Jesus said would not be a great moral teacher. He would either be a lunatic—on a level with the man who says he is a poached egg— or else he would be the Devil of Hell. You must make your choice. Either this man was, and is, the Son of God: or else a madman or something worse. . . . But let us not come up with any patronizing nonsense about His being a great human teacher. He has not left that open to us. He did not intend to."*

---

* C. S. Lewis, *Mere Christianity* (New York: HarperCollins, 2001), p. 52.

LESSON 4

HIS OWN TESTIMONY

Key Texts: *Daniel 7:13, 14; Matthew 17:1–9; 26:62–66; Mark 8:27–38; Luke 1:34, 35; John 8:48–59; 10:19–33; 14:8, 9; Philippians 2:9–11*

What titles did Jesus claim for Himself?
What titles do I accept as belonging to Jesus?
What do the titles of Jesus imply for my relationship with Him?

This week's memory text: *"Therefore God also has highly exalted Him and given Him the name which is above every name, that at the name of Jesus every knee should bow, of those in heaven, and of those on earth, and of those under the earth, and that every tongue should confess that Jesus Christ is **Lord**, to the glory of God the Father"* (Phil. 2:9–11, NKJV).

KEY TERMS

Lord—This title carries a variety of meanings from supreme master to any person with authority. Meaning must be determined by context and the original Hebrew or Greek word. Sometimes it was used simply as a term of respect, like "sir." When the early Christians used "Lord" with the name of Jesus, the title carried the highest possible meaning. (See "Confession of faith" on page 34.)

Sunday

Last week's lesson surveyed the titles that others used when speaking to or about Jesus. This week's lesson will consider the titles that Jesus claimed for Himself. In the process, we will begin to observe how Jesus taught His disciples and what He expects of them. One of His teaching challenges was to correct some misunderstandings that the disciples had absorbed through their culture. As we hear Jesus correcting His disciples, we might profitably reflect on how our own culture has distorted our understanding of who Jesus is.

Walking With Jesus in the Real World

An Atheist's Hostility Toward Christians—*Sergei Datskovsky**

My parents, grandmother, and I immigrated to the United States from the former Soviet Union. We had been indoctrinated with atheism from an early age, but a tension existed because we are Jewish. In the States, my parents sent me to a Jewish religious school. I left after a few years because neither my parents nor I believed what the school taught.

Going to public school in Brooklyn quickly helped me forget about God. Until college, I rarely thought about God. Then two things changed—both for the worse. First, some of the science professors taught that human beings are the product of evolution and that there is no Creator. This broke down what little belief I had in God. Second, I started to get involved in the New Age movement, and this made me hostile toward Christians.

My thought process from atheism to Christianity was a slow journey. First, I had several frightening experiences with the New Age movement that made me back away from it. But that left me feeling spiritually empty. I explored different religions and belief systems, but none of them seemed right. It was about this time that I met my wife-to-be, Ann. Originally, I became interested in her because of her beauty, but when I spoke to her I discovered that there was more to her than just that. I found myself drawn to her calmness and thoughtfulness.

When I got to know Ann, I discovered that she was a Christian and belonged to a group that keeps the Sabbath. To find out more about this group, I borrowed a bunch of books from her library. I found writers like C. S. Lewis and Ellen White to be very different from what I expected. These were very thoughtful people who had good reasons for what they believed. I still wasn't convinced; I wanted hard evidence.

That evidence came when I visited Ann's home in the Midwest and sat in on her stepdad's Sabbath School class. Bill was teaching the 490-year prophecy in the book of Daniel. When I saw that the prophecy fit perfectly with history, I was amazed. Through my own research, I confirmed what he had taught. This sparked an interest in the Bible. Bill offered to study the Bible with me over the phone each week and I accepted. Each new lesson strengthened my faith and before long I was baptized.

I won't say it was an easy decision. I am a Jew and there is strong pressure from within the Jewish community (religious and secular) not to convert to Christianity. I decided, however, that it is better to follow your convictions, even if it means alienating friends and even family.

I'm grateful that God had the mercy to reach me while I was still young so that I didn't spend my life looking for satisfaction and never finding it. Jesus said that unless a man is born again, he cannot enter the kingdom of heaven. He also said that the kingdom of heaven is within us.

And so it is with my life. When I became a Christian, I died to my old life and now live a new life with Christ. Day by day He changes me from the inside out, and He has given me a purpose to my life that I never had before. So I can truly say that the kingdom of heaven is now within me and that living for Christ is a down payment on eternity.

* A pseudonym.

MESSIAH

The account of an important teaching event appears about midway through the Gospel of Mark. It reports something about who Jesus is, but it also shows how Jesus teaches His disciples and something of what He expects of them. In first-century Israel, the typical teaching method of rabbis was to answer questions asked by their disciples. In this teaching session, as Mark reports it, Jesus reverses the practice and asks His disciples a question. Read the story carefully to discover several important teachings of Jesus. Read Mark 8:27–38.

• What question did Jesus ask?

• Who answered?

• What was his answer?

   Last week's lesson indicates that the title "Christ" is the Greek term for what Hebrew title?

   Jesus responded in an unusual way by warning them to tell no one about Him. That instruction is the opposite of what might be expected since it is vital for people to know who Jesus is. We'll consider this a little later. Jesus used this occasion, however, to begin teaching the disciples something very central to His mission. What did He explain about Himself? Read Mark 8:31, 32.

• How did Peter react to the teaching?

   It may seem that Peter spoke out of his love for Jesus, that he did not want that kind of future for Jesus. How did Jesus interpret Peter's comment?

   Peter's idea of what the Messiah should be and should do reflected what his culture thought of the Messiah—that the Messiah would free the country from foreign rule. There was no understanding that the Messiah would suffer and die. The two ideas of the Messiah as a conquering ruler *and* a suffering martyr seemed contradictory. Although Peter's understanding of Jesus' identity was more accurate than that of the crowd, it was still incomplete. The crowd's faulty understanding, which was shaped by their cultural hopes for the Messiah, helps to explain why Jesus, at this time, did not want His disciples announcing to everyone that He was the Messiah. Imagine the political unrest that such an announcement would have caused. Jesus' real mission would have been lost in the chaos.

IMPLICATIONS OF THE SUFFERING MESSIAH

Immediately after that strange scene in which Jesus said to Peter, "Get behind me, Satan," because Peter did not want Jesus to suffer and be killed, Jesus gathered the disciples and others around Him and began to teach them the most important lesson on how to be one of His disciples. Read Mark 8:34. What three things does Jesus say a disciple must do?

1.

2.

3.

• What do these instructions mean for how you live your life?

How appealing are these instructions? How could an advertising company create a commercial to promote this kind of life? In these instructions we see a basic principle that Jesus had just spoken to Peter in the preceding verse: God's viewpoint is not the same as the human viewpoint. Goals are different; values are different. In the next few verses, Jesus begins to explain why a disciple must live the way He has just described and what is at stake. Read Mark 8:35–38. What remarkable "law of life" does Jesus reveal?

Some have termed it the law of the "upside-down kingdom of God." It's all about the focus of your life. A graduate student, who was researching discipleship at a major university with ties to a Christian denomination, went to her dissertation advisor and explained that she was having difficulty trying to explain the heart of discipleship and even trying to understand what it should look like in her own life. The advisor listened and then said, "The problem is, you are thinking in terms of 'Jesus and . . .' 'Jesus and my ambitions.' 'Jesus and my reputation.' 'Jesus and my salary.' 'Jesus and my husband.' Discipleship is just 'Jesus.' "

HOW JESUS DESCRIBED HIMSELF

During His days with His disciples, Jesus frequently pointed out misconceptions people had about God and about His promises and expectations for His people. In Monday's portion of this week's lesson, we learned that Jesus had to correct the people's understanding of the term *Messiah*. In His explanation, He used His favorite title for Himself.

Read again Mark 8:31, 38. What is the title?
Notice that this title is associated with different things in the two verses.

• What is the title associated with in verse 31?

• In verse 38?

Those in Jesus' time who heard Jesus use the title "Son of Man" pictured something very definite coming from two characters described in the prophecies of Isaiah and Daniel. In Isaiah, there is a large section that refers to a Suffering Servant. The most famous passage is Isaiah 53 (with the title "servant" being introduced in the preceding verses of Isaiah 52:13–15). Read Isaiah 53 and think about some of the reasons that Jesus chose a title linked to suffering.

Suffering and servanthood are not the only concepts related to the title "Son of Man," as Mark 8:38 points out. Read Daniel 7:13, 14. What are the characteristics of the One who is "like the Son of Man"?

Jesus used the term "Son of Man" to refer to Himself more than any other title. It is a rich term with deep meaning that can be found in the writings of the Old Testament prophets. It also gives two dramatically different views of Jesus. The disciples (except Judas) witnessed Jesus as the Suffering, Dying Servant; Peter, James, and John saw Christ glorified at the **Transfiguration** (Matt. 17:1–9). Stephen, the first martyr, saw the glorified Son of Man in vision (Acts 7:55, 56). So did John in Revelation 1:9–17.

ADVENTESE

Members of the Seventh-day Adventist Church meet together in several kinds of gatherings.

• **Worship, "11 o'clock hour," "Divine service":** The entire congregation gathers on Sabbath morning for worship, which most commonly includes music, the oral reading of Scripture, the collection of an offering, and a sermon.

• **Vespers or Sundown Worship:** A worship meeting that usually begins shortly before sundown on Friday to welcome the Sabbath and on Saturday to close the Sabbath.

• **Week of Prayer:** Two times a year, a week is set aside for special prayer meetings. Weeks of Prayer are also held on all Adventist academy and college campuses.

• **Camp meeting:** Camp meetings are weeklong summer gatherings of Adventists who live within a conference. These meetings, designed for spiritual nourishment, are usually held on academy campuses or at the conference's camp. Historically, these meetings spanned two weekends and the week between. Some conferences have now shortened the time.

KEY TERMS

Transfiguration—The change that made Jesus appear as a figure of brilliant splendor.

THE ULTIMATE CLAIM

Even though the term "sons of God" had been in use for a long time, the title "Son of God" took on a unique meaning with the appearance of Jesus. What were the circumstances at the earliest time this title was applied to Jesus? Read Luke 1:34, 35.

What evidence do we have that even as a child Jesus sensed His special relationship to God? Read Luke 2:41–50.

Because of the power and authority demonstrated by Jesus and His popularity with the people, His identity was of great interest to the Jewish leaders. In a dramatic exchange with the Pharisees when Jesus talks about His Father " 'whom you claim as your God,' " they responded by trying to stone Him (John 8:54, NIV). Read John 8:48–59. What other claim did Jesus make at this time that inflamed the Jews?

Later when the controversy over Jesus' identity erupted again, what claim did Jesus make regarding His relationship to His Father? Read John 10:19–30.

Why did that make the Jews so angry that they took up stones again to stone Him? Read verses 31–33.

Monday's portion of this lesson examined how important it was to Jesus that He correct the disciples' understanding of the title "Messiah." Last week's lesson recounted times when others called Him "Son of God," yet He never corrected them. Jesus Himself did not use the title, but once under oath He testified that the title was accurate. Read Matthew 26:62–66. What price did Jesus pay for claiming the title "Son of God"?

The Jews knew that Jesus was claiming divinity; this they could not accept. In spite of the danger, Jesus did not try to soften His bold claim. The title "Son of God" is so central to His identity that He was willing to die for it. John 14:8, 9 shows the significance of this title to His disciples—to us. Jesus, who is both Son of man and Son of God, is the only One who can reveal God to us. He is "God with us."

Friday

CHECKING UP

1. Which title was most frequently used by Jesus to refer to Himself?
   A. Messiah
   B. Son of Man
   C. Son of God
2. Which title led to the crucifixion of Jesus?
   A. Messiah
   B. Son of Man
   C. Son of God
3. Why was it important that the disciples not go about proclaiming that Jesus was the Messiah? (Circle all that apply.)
   A. People had a misunderstanding of what the Messiah would do.
   B. Jesus did not consider Himself to be the Messiah.
   C. If the people would have thought that Jesus was the Messiah, they would probably have caused a great political upheaval.
   D. The people would have expected all kinds of material benefits from Jesus and would have missed the eternal life He came to give them.

Extend Your Learning

This week's memory text is part of what many scholars believe was an early Christian hymn that Paul adapted and used as a **confession of faith** in his letter to the Philippians. Few people in Paul's time could read. Learning was accomplished through memorization and often through "psalms and hymns and spiritual songs" (Col. 3:16, NKJV). Memorize the entire hymn found in Philippians 2:5–11. Some Bible translations print the hymn in poetic format.

Examine Your Own Experience

In Mark 8:34, Jesus clearly stated three requirements for being a disciple. The first requirement is to "deny" yourself. This instruction is commonly misunderstood to mean that you should deny yourself the pleasures of life, even necessities.

But Jesus does not mean that. He says to deny the self. As a disciple, you will be willing to give up anything that separates you from Christ or from His will for you. You give up your natural desire to be self-centered. What self-centered attitudes and behaviors in your own life need to be denied?

More resources on this topic can be found at http://www.InStepWithJesus.org/Journey.

KEY TERMS

Confession of faith—A personal and public declaration of faith. The earliest confession of faith was "Jesus is Lord." By this, Christians meant that the Jesus of history is the risen Christ of faith, that Christ is God, and that He has absolute supremacy in the universe, the church, and individual lives.*

---

* Geoffrey Bromiley, ed., *The International Bible Encyclopedia* (Grand Rapids, Mich.: Eerdmans, 1979), CD-ROM.

More on What People Today Think of Jesus

If you never went to church and never listened to a sermon and never read your Bible, how would you learn about Jesus? What would you think of Him? You would probably get your information about Him from popular culture: television, movies, books, or the Internet. Sometimes the media gets it right; at other times, they do not.

Googling the name "Jesus Christ" will currently produce about 30 million entries. The views of Jesus at these Web sites will range from "He is an imaginary figure" to "He is God." People choose to believe the Jesus that fits their worldview. If they hold a naturalist philosophy (only the material world exists), the highest opinion that is possible for them to have of Jesus is that He was the wisest, kindest human being who ever lived.

A group of about 150 people, many of whom are—incredibly—scholars in biblical and religious studies (yet who do not believe Jesus rose from the dead), meet twice a year to vote with colored beads to decide which of Jesus' words and deeds recorded in the Gospels are historically true. To them Jesus was only a wise Jewish rabbi.

On the other hand, a large percentage of the general American population believes Jesus to be the Son of God. But a new perspective about Jesus has been developing in recent years. Because the culture is influenced by postmodernism (a perspective that there is no such thing as objective reality and that one belief is as good as another belief), Christians who believe that Jesus Christ is unique and the only One worthy of worship are considered rigid, dogmatic, and intolerant. Almost anyone in today's culture is willing for you to believe that Jesus is the Son of God, but don't try to convince them of that fact if they don't already believe it.

When it comes to understanding Jesus, you can't depend on your culture to get it right.

A Closer Look

Significance of "I AM."

The Jews of Jesus' time felt superior to all other people because they could claim Abraham, the recipient of God's special blessing, to be their father. Once in a heated discussion with Jesus, they responded to a cryptic statement He had made by saying, " 'You are not yet fifty years old, and have You seen Abraham?' Jesus said to them, 'Most assuredly, I say to you, before Abraham was, I AM' " (John 8:57, 58, NKJV).

The words "I AM" so infuriated the Jews that they picked up stones to throw at Jesus, but He escaped. Why did those two simple words so upset the Jews? The answer to that question refers to the story of Moses and the burning bush. Read Exodus 3:13, 14.

When God spoke to Moses from the burning bush and told him to go to Egypt and free His people, Moses asked God what His name is. And God said that His name is "I AM."

The Jews knew that Jesus was claiming to be God. And in their culture, that was blasphemy, punishable by death.

Key Terms

Blasphemy—Insulting or showing contempt for God. In the Old Testament, this was punishable with death by stoning.

MY UPSIDE-DOWN WORLD

Key Texts: *Matthew 23:1–13, 25–28; Luke 24:13–35; John 3:1–21; 4:4–15; 7:45–52; 19:38–42*

Why has becoming a disciple turned my world upside down? How does the Word of God challenge every worldview? What happens when my worldview changes, but the worldviews of my family and friends do not?

This week's memory text: *"Then He said to them, 'O foolish ones, and slow of heart to believe in all that the prophets have spoken! Ought not the Christ to have suffered these things and to enter into His glory?'"* (Luke 24:25, 26, NKJV).

KEY TERMS

Worldview—Worldview is the lens through which we understand our world. It consists of the assumptions (whether they are true or not) we have (whether we are conscious of them or not) about the basic reality of the world and life. We absorb these assumptions from our family, the media, and the culture we live in. When we change our worldview, we change our perspective on one or more major issues.

Disciples of Jesus have a worldview that differs from the worldview of secular people or people from other religions or even from the worldview of nominal (in name only) Christians.

The memory text this week is taken from a story of Jesus leading two disciples through a worldview change. Wherever the story of Jesus is preached, it causes a conflict in the predominant worldview. In one instance as the early Christians preached the gospel in a Greek city, the Jews dragged them before the city rulers and condemned them with these words, " 'These who have turned the world upside down have come here too' " (Acts 17:6, NKJV).

Walking With Jesus in the Real World

Escaping Empty Narratives—*John Schneider*

I have attended Adventist schools all my life. I wasn't a rebellious student, so I just sat back and was spoon-fed. Yet near the end of my first year in college, I decided to spend the next year as a student missionary.

For ten months I taught in a mission school on a small, remote island in the Pacific. It wasn't a typical tropical island. My island was one mile long, 300 yards wide, and 8 feet above sea level at the highest point. Eighty percent of its 15,000 residents were under the age of 20. It is, according to *National Geographic,* "the armpit of the Pacific." Of the student body, only 5 percent were Adventist students. Beer and cigarettes were making their mark. Sexual promiscuity reigned. Most young people wanted to leave the island, but only the very rich or very intelligent managed to do that.

We student missionaries faced a huge job. How could we give these students hope and meaning in life? Over the course of that year, I became filled with gratitude that God could use me to be an example and build relationships that could give hope to some of the students.

When I finished the year and returned home, my siblings came home to welcome me back. A couple of days later, my oldest brother suggested that we go to an amusement park. Two hours into our day there, I could be amused no longer. The experience contrasted too dramatically with the life that I had just left. I could not relate to the need for this false fulfillment. Some call what I was going through reverse culture shock. I now call it "welcome back to the land of empty narratives."

In the fall I returned to college and over the next four years I somehow slipped back into my pre–Pacific island life as a "comfortably numb" Christian. I had returned to being spoon-fed. When I graduated, I began work as a church school teacher. I was a good teacher, committed to my students. But my personal life was hollow—without purpose or meaning. At times I felt as though I couldn't be any farther away from God. How could this be? Teaching at a Christian school?

I was fortunate that Jesus was seeking me, and through some turn of events, I entered an Adventist university to work on my master's degree with the hope that I would find something to rejuvenate my suffering, perhaps nonexistent, spiritual life. One of the class requirements was to read a book titled *Finding God at Harvard.* The writers who contributed to the book shared their struggles and how Christ sustained and enabled them. The book moved me deeply. A requirement to listen to audio tapes brought me into contact with speakers who defended their Christian faith with gripping clarity.

It was exactly what I needed to hear, at exactly the right time. Throughout the weeks of the classes, the culturally induced cataracts were removed from my worldview. Faith and clarity of purpose and meaning returned. Because of the class and my openness to the Holy Spirit, I began building a relationship with Jesus. Finally, there was no other satisfying option.

HOW RADICAL IS THE WORLDVIEW OF JESUS?

To avoid being seen by his associates, Nicodemus, a teacher and member of the Jewish ruling council, came to Jesus under the cover of darkness, probably to discuss spiritual issues. The discussion did not go as he had planned. Read John 3:1–21.

Based on Nicodemus's opening comment, who did he think Jesus was and what did he hope to accomplish by his comment?

• Who was Jesus actually?

• What was the purpose of Nicodemus's comment?

• What was Jesus' response to Nicodemus's comment that caught Nicodemus off guard?

Nicodemus, socially prominent and highly educated, felt secure before God because as a Jew he was a child of Abraham, the favored of God. But Jesus said that his natural birth as a descendant of Abraham would not even let him "see" the kingdom of God. Nicodemus needed to be born again—from a different Source. According to Jesus, how does the new birth happen? Read John 3:5–8.

Instead of entering into an intellectual discussion with Nicodemus, Jesus shattered his worldview by telling him that his Jewish heritage and his outward religious practices were worthless in God's kingdom. He needed to repent and to experience a total change of heart. Then the Gospel writer John records the profound teaching that Jesus gave to Nicodemus. What John does not tell us is how Nicodemus responded.

To change one's worldview is not a simple matter. It takes time to reconsider all of one's assumptions. Nicodemus appears in the Gospel two more times. Based on these two incidents, how do you think Nicodemus eventually responded to Jesus' shocking comments during the night visit? Read John 7:45–52; 19:38–42.

Tuesday

BREAKING DOWN BARRIERS

Few stories in the Gospels are given as much space (41 verses) as the story of Jesus' interaction with the woman of **Samaria**. To read of this incident more than 2,000 years after it happened and possibly thousands of miles from where it happened means that we are reading it from a twenty-first-century worldview. But to understand the real drama, we need to understand the first-century Jewish and Samaritan worldview. Read John 4:4–9.

What two characteristics of the woman showed that Jesus was breaking down barriers in the prevalent worldview?

1.

2.

The conversation begins with a discussion of water. Read John 4:10–15. Both the woman and Jesus had water to offer to each other. How did these two types of water differ?

The conversation ends with Jesus telling the woman that He is the Messiah. During the conversation, He had pointed out that she was a sinner. How did she respond to this blunt disclosure? Scholars believe that the woman had come to the well at a time when no one else was around because she was probably a social outcast. What clues does the end of the story provide about the woman's response to Jesus? Read John 4:39–42.

It is probably safe to say that all books that explain Jesus' teaching methods include a detailed discussion of how He taught this Samaritan woman. At the same time, He was also teaching someone else—His disciples. And He was specifically teaching for the purpose of transforming their worldview. The disciples returned from their food shopping excursion just as the conversation between Jesus and the woman was ending. Read John 4:4, 27. In what sense did Jesus "need" to go through Samaria?

• What changes was Jesus trying to make in the disciples' worldview?

KEY TERMS

Samaria—A region north of Judah. The religion of the people of Samaria, Samaritans, had become corrupted through pagan influences.

FROM OUTWARD BEHAVIOR TO INWARD CHANGE

In the world of Jesus' time, the Pharisees were the conservative religious party and hostile to Jesus and His teachings. They thought He was undermining the laws of Moses, and they often set verbal traps to prove it. Read of one encounter between Jesus and the Pharisees and teachers of the law in Matthew 23:1–13, 25–28. What did the Pharisees and teachers value?

• What did Jesus apparently value?

The numerous religious rules of the Pharisees kept the people in a continuous state of anxiety, wondering, *Am I good enough to enter the kingdom of God?*

Jesus began His preaching ministry with the message, " 'Repent, for the kingdom of heaven is at hand' " (Matt. 4:17, NKJV). In His great **sermon on the mount**, Jesus explained the nature of that kingdom. The disciples and the surrounding crowd listened in amazement to His words that shattered the worldview created by their religious leaders.

He begins with blessings, which are called "the Beatitudes." (See "A Closer Look" on page 41.) There is no recorded evidence in all of the New Testament that the Pharisees ever blessed anyone.

The law says . . .	But I say . . .
Matthew 5:21, 22	
Matthew 5:27, 28	
Matthew 5:38, 39	
Matthew 5:43, 44	

Describe the change in worldview that Jesus was making.

KEY TERMS

Sermon on the Mount—This is the first and longest of five sermons, or formal talks, by Jesus as recorded in the Gospel of Matthew. It describes the kingdom that Jesus came to introduce and shows the differences between His teachings and the traditions that had built up around Jewish law. The reaction of the people who first heard the Sermon on the Mount was one of astonishment at Jesus' authority. See Matthew 7:28, 29.

Thursday
FROM SADNESS TO JOY

Human beings face disappointments in life. When the disappointment comes from the most important thing in their lives, it can be devastating. The crucifixion of Jesus was devastating to the disciples who, believing He was the Messiah, had left all to follow Him.

In Luke 24:13–35, read a story that details the sadness of two disciples grieving over the death of Jesus and that shows how the sadness turned to joy.

• What was the heart of their sadness or disappointment? Read verses 14, 19–24.

• What were they doing to try to explain the situation? Read verses 14, 25–27.

• What incident opened their eyes? Read verses 30, 31.

• What was their emotional reaction to this insight? Read verse 32.

• What did they do with the news? Read verses 33–35.

With their new insight and understanding, the two disciples were eager to tell the other disciples. It is interesting, however, that they did not get to report the news to the eleven disciples. Instead, they were met at the door with the excited words "It's true! The Lord has risen and has appeared to Simon." Although it must have been a little disappointing not to be able to surprise the Eleven with their news, the experience of Simon and their experience served to establish the truth of what they had experienced. This new understanding of the Messiah changed their worldview.

A CLOSER LOOK

The Beatitudes (Matt. 5:3–10)

In Matthew's record of the Sermon on the Mount, Jesus begins with eight blessings, which have been named the Beatitudes. The word Jesus uses for "blessed" means "happy." It is obvious that the kingdom Jesus was talking about is far different from any kingdom of this world. It is especially puzzling to consider as happy the "poor in spirit," "those who mourn," and the "persecuted."

To rightly understand the blessings, you have to realize that Jesus is describing those who have rejected the values of this world and have submitted to the will of God.

- "Poor in spirit" means they recognize their spiritual poverty.
- "Those who mourn" are those who grieve over their sins and the evil in the world.
- Happiness is possible, even in persecution, when the Christian experiences the peace of God's love.

True blessedness, or happiness, comes from living within the kingdom of God.

Friday

CHECKING UP

1. After Jesus shattered Nicodemus's worldview, how did Nicodemus respond? (Circle the letters of all that apply.)
   A. Immediately became a disciple
   B. Privately pondered what Jesus had said
   C. Became a public disciple after Jesus' death

2. What emotion did the woman at the well experience at the conclusion of her encounter with Jesus?
   A. Embarrassment
   B. Anger
   C. Joy

3. In the sections we read of the Sermon on the Mount, what changes in perspective was Jesus trying to give the people? (Circle the letters of all that apply.)
   A. From the letter of the law to the spirit of the law
   B. From outward behavior to inward attitude
   C. From thinking He had come to abolish the law to knowing that He fulfilled it

Examine Your Own Experience

As a new member of the Seventh-day Adventist Church, you have probably been experiencing changes in your worldview. Which of the following beliefs have had an impact on your worldview? (Check all that apply.)

____ We are saved through faith in Jesus and not because we have earned salvation.
____ God loves us even when we sin.
____ People do not immediately go to heaven or hell when they die.
____ God will not burn the unsaved in hell forever.
____ The seventh-day Sabbath (Saturday) is still to be kept holy.
____ Living a healthful lifestyle is one aspect of honoring God.
____ When Jesus returns to this earth, He will raise the dead.

Discuss this question with your study group: When family and friends do not share your new views, how do they react? What are appropriate ways for you to respond?

More resources on this topic can be found at http://www.InStepWithJesus.org/Journey.

Learning That Transforms

Much of human learning is like addition. We add to what we know about carpentry or cooking, about our careers or our hobbies, about being parents or grandparents. But some learning is like an explosion. When the debris settles, we realize the landscape has changed. This explosive kind of learning is called transformational learning. And it is the kind of learning that the disciples experienced from the fallout of the crucifixion and resurrection of Jesus.

This is also the kind of learning you probably experienced as you began to understand who Jesus is and what He has done for you. It is the learning that occurs when your eyes are opened to the contrast between what your culture values and what God values. Transformational learning is what Paul was encouraging when he wrote, "Do not be conformed to this world, but be transformed by the renewing of your mind" (Rom. 12:2, NKJV).

Transformational learning changes your most deeply held beliefs or assumptions—sometimes your worldview. It changes the lens through which you see everything. Because of the importance of transformational learning, many people have studied it, trying to figure out how it happens. Here is the way one educator has described how we are changed by what we learn:*

1. You experience a "crisis" or "disorienting dilemma," for example, with a tragic or disappointing experience or with something you hear or read that your current perspective cannot explain or help you endure.

2. During the search for an answer, you try to resolve the dilemma. Your mind attempts to find an explanation. This can last only minutes—or years.

3. The "aha moment" comes when you suddenly gain insight into the dilemma; you find a solution and experience a sense of relief or a sense that your world has been put back together again. In spiritual matters, this is when the Holy Spirit gives new understanding.

4. The final step is interpretation and verification. Now, with your new perspective, you interpret your life in a new way, looking differently at your experiences and beliefs, both current and past. You also look to others to affirm the truthfulness of your new understanding.

Can you identify transforming experiences that you have had? How closely did they follow this pattern?

ADVENTESE

Seventh-day Adventists use several terms in their worship services.

• **Altar call:** The invitation (usually "to accept Christ as Savior") at the end of a sermon for people to indicate commitment by walking forward to the pulpit.

• **Communion service or Lord's Supper:** Symbolic meal commemorating Jesus' death. Typically performed once each quarter, it consists of a short sermon, footwashing, and the blessing and partaking of the bread and wine (grape juice) by all baptized believers.

• **Footwashing or Ordinance of Humility:** A ritual washing of another believer's feet as part of the Communion service.

• **Thirteenth Sabbath:** The last Sabbath of each quarter of the year; marked by a special program in the Sabbath School, especially by the children; larger than usual offering is given for missions.

* James E. Loder, *The Transforming Moment*, 2nd ed. (Colorado Springs, Colo.: Helmers and Howard, 1989), pp. 2–4.

GOD'S PRIORITIES—AND MINE

Key Texts: *Genesis 1:26–31; 2:16, 17; Matthew 4:18–20; 6:31–34; 19:16–26; 22:37–40; Luke 2:8–11; 9:59–62; 14:25–33; John 3:16; 10:10*

What are my highest priorities?
How do my priorities relate to God's priorities for me?
What should I do with my life?

This week's memory text: " *'I have come that they may have life, and that they may have it more abundantly'* " (John 10:10, NKJV).

Sunday

When a guest appears on a television talk show, there are certain things that he or she can say and guarantee an immediate and approving applause from the audience. One of those lines is, "I just want my child to be happy." (Applause!)

Happiness. Should happiness be our highest priority? We certainly would not choose *unhappiness* as a priority for our lives. This lesson will explore God's priorities for human beings and consider what it would mean if we were to make His priorities our own.

Walking With Jesus in the Real World

Ministering in the Nuts and Bolts Aisle—*Dick Gardner**

For a whole year they tried to find a place to work in an overseas mission field, but no one needed their particular combination of skills. With Dick's building and maintenance experience, he could have worked anywhere. His wife, Pam, however, had just earned a degree in physical therapy, a medical specialty that is rarely sought in mission work.

Is God wanting us to buy a hardware store? they wondered. This question was not as strange as it sounds. In college Dick had worked part time doing maintenance for a local entrepreneur who owned several small businesses. His frequent trips to hardware stores to buy parts made him aware of the need for a hardware store that would have an extensive stock of common repair items and that would be open long hours.

After considering several options, he and Pam bought the inventory and shelving of an old hardware store that had been in the small town for 100 years, but had fallen on hard times in competition with the "big box" stores. The owner of the building gave them a good deal on the rent. Then they closed the store for three months to clean it up and refinish the ceiling and floors.

For the first few years, the young couple lived on Pam's salary. Although the business was closed on Saturday, it slowly grew. When they needed more space, they bought a larger building down the street and moved the business. Several employees now work for them.

Those who know him wonder if Dick plans to spend the rest of his career as the owner/manager of a hardware store. "I majored in marketing. If I wanted to work in marketing, I'd have to go to Chicago or New York and climb the corporate ladder," he says. "That's not the life for me. We just take it a day at a time and wait to see what God has in mind."

Dick explains his perspective on his hardware business: "Our whole purpose in this business is to make it a ministry. The fact that we sell hardware is a sideline. We spend a lot of time in the aisles listening to people. While we help them find things, we hear about their troubles—'I need parts to fix my toilet, but I don't have any money,' or 'My marriage isn't doing well.' We have a huge base of people who come in regularly to buy something, to get the free popcorn, and to talk.

"If this is all it is—selling hardware—it wouldn't be worth it. There's never enough money. Someone is always selling for less. But all day is a witnessing opportunity. This store is a secret front for the Lord to work through us."

Dick's customers might be surprised to hear this. He is a laid-back, quiet person who just comes across as a nice guy.

_____
* A pseudonym.

WHOSE PRIORITIES?

If we were to determine human values based on the salaries that people in various professions or occupations earn, what would emerge as among the highest priorities? How would you rank these occupations by salary: teacher, sports star, movie actor, farmer, mother/childcare giver, secretary, refugee camp worker, investment banker, and factory worker. Of the types of people listed, which provide the most important services to human beings? Do people who perform the most important services receive the highest salaries?

It is probably safe to say that one of the highest priorities of human beings is earning money and being able to purchase all that it can buy. Among other priorities are obtaining the esteem of others, wielding power, enjoying close relationships with others, and retaining a healthy mind and body.

What would you name as God's highest priorities? Christians believe that in the life of Jesus we can learn more about God and His values than through any other source. Very early in His life, the purpose of Jesus was revealed. Read Luke 2:8–11. When was Jesus' purpose announced?

• What was that purpose?

Much later Jesus explained the purpose for which His Father sent Him. Read John 3:16. What was God's purpose for sending Jesus to earth?

• What did Jesus say was His purpose for coming to earth? Read John 10:10.

The Psalms have been the song and prayer book of Jews and Christians for hundreds of years. They record in poetic form the responses of human beings to God. They are full of emotion expressing joy, praise, fear, anger, hope, love, and faith. Often a single psalm will express several emotions. In some of the psalms, you can see a person struggling to get his priorities right. Read Psalm 27. What is the one thing that David asked of the Lord?

It surely doesn't mean that he wants to stay in the temple all his life. What could it mean?

God wants to give us an abundant life now and throughout eternity. How do you think God would describe an abundant life? Is it the same way you would describe it?

THE LONG VIEW

Understanding how God would describe "an abundant life" should begin at the beginning. When God created human beings, what did He have in mind for them? Read Genesis 1:26–31.

In addition to providing all that Adam and Eve needed, God gave them the ability to choose—or reject—God's plan (Gen. 2:16, 17). What interrupted God's plan? Read the story in Genesis 3.

This story gives a glimpse of how sin changed Adam and Eve's relationship with God. What must that relationship have been like before their sin? Read verse 8.

Only two chapters in the entire Bible (Genesis 1 and 2) give us information about life on earth before sin changed the world. And only two chapters (Revelation 21 and 22) give us a glimpse into what life will be like *after* this earth has been restored: Eden and Eden restored. The rest of the story, the huge middle, tells how God is working out His plans to **redeem** and **restore** human beings. This is God's top priority—redeeming and restoring human beings. Every other good thing is only secondary.

When Jesus called His disciples, He was asking them to join Him in His work of redemption and restoration. What metaphor did Jesus use to describe this work? Read Matthew 4:18–20.

Our highest purpose is to partner with Jesus in His work. We have been made in the **image of God** and invited by Jesus to join Him in His work. Our highest priority should be to partner with God as He creates, redeems, and restores. Happiness will be a by-product. How can we do these things?

KEY TERMS

Redeem—Through Christ's death for our sins, we are put back into a right relationship with God.

Restore—"This process of salvation removes 'the old self' and creates a 'new self.' . . . Paul speaks of this new person as one renewed in knowledge, holiness, and righteousness (Col. 3:10; Eph. 4:21-24). . . . By implication we may affirm that the original image of God must have constituted knowledge, holiness, and righteousness."*

Image of God—Contrary to evolutionary theory, human beings are not simply the highest form of animals. We share a likeness to God. What constitutes this likeness is not fully understood, but in Genesis we see that God gave humans dominion, abilities to think and create and to have relationships with Him and each other, and freedom of choice. (See "Restore.")

---

* John M. Fowler, *Handbook of Seventh-day Adventist Theology* (Hagerstown, Md.: Review and Herald® Publishing Association, 2000), p. 235.

Wednesday

DISTORTED PRIORITIES

We are familiar with the men who accepted Jesus' invitation to follow Him to become the twelve disciples. But there were others who wanted to be disciples, but who did not want following Jesus to be their first priority. Read Matthew 19:16–26. What reason is given for the young man's decision not to follow Jesus?

What principle did Jesus teach His disciples based on this encounter with the young man? Read verses 23, 24.

There are at least two other examples of people who were not willing to "leave all." What excuse did each give and what was Jesus' response? Read Luke 9:59–62.

Excuse:
Jesus' comment:

Excuse:
Jesus' comment:

The most challenging of all Jesus' statements about becoming a disciple occurs in His description of the cost of being a disciple. Read Luke 14:25–33. How unlike modern marketers Jesus was! He did not pretend that difficult things were easy. He tells people to count the cost. In this teaching, Jesus makes a startling statement about human relationships. What is that statement? Read verse 26.

How does this statement fit into what you know about Jesus? See the sidebar on this page.

The cost of being a disciple is not the same for everyone. Jesus is really dealing with priorities. He is not opposed to wealth; He is opposed to wealth being a person's highest priority. He is not opposed to close human relationships; He is opposed to human relationships that are more important than a relationship with Him.

In the Sermon on the Mount, Jesus explains the relationship between priorities and human needs. What is that relationship? Read Matthew 6:31–34.

A CLOSER LOOK

"A Hard Saying"

When Jesus says that we cannot be His disciples unless we " 'hate [our] father and mother, wife and children, brothers and sisters' " (Luke 14:26, NKJV), it is shocking to our contemporary ears.

To understand this teaching, we must take into account that the people of Jesus' time may differ from us in the way they expressed ideas. In Luke 16:13, Jesus said, " 'No servant can serve two masters; for either he will hate the one and love the other, or else he will be loyal to the one and despise the other' " (NKJV). In both texts Jesus is telling us that it is impossible to serve two masters. One must be given priority, and He must be that One.

"A person who commits himself or herself to Christ will develop a greater love for both neighbor and family, although at times loving and following Christ may be seen as renunciation, rejection, or hate if the family does not share the same commitment to Christ."*

* Robert H. Stein, *The New American Commentary* (Nashville: Baptist Sunday School Board, 2002).

LIVING GOD'S PRIORITIES AS MY OWN

Dietrich Bonhoeffer knew the cost of discipleship. He paid the full price when he was executed in 1945 for his beliefs. Earlier he had written, "Christianity without discipleship is always Christianity without Christ."*

Being a follower of Jesus Christ will change your life, not just because of the one, dramatic decision to follow Him, but day by day as you learn more about His love for you and His will for your life. As a disciple following Jesus and partnering with Him in His mission, you understand that your life gets its meaning from serving others. "Serving others" is a shortened way to say in broad terms that you are helping to redeem and restore people, organizations, law, etc., and even things of nature—and doing all this with all the creative power that you have as a person created in the image of God.

Understanding this purpose always raises the question, What should I do with my life? Jesus summarized this issue in answer to a question someone asked about obtaining eternal life. Read Matthew 22:37–40. According to this statement, what should your choices allow you to do?

Those twin concerns of love for God and love for human beings are reminders of what the Old Testament prophet Micah said about the purpose of life. What words does Micah use? Read Micah 6:8.

Are you concerned that the call of Jesus to follow Him will take you where you don't want to go? "The kind of work God usually calls you to is the kind of work that you need most to do and that the world most needs to have done. . . . The place God calls you to is the place where your deep gladness and the world's deep hunger meet."† There you will find the abundant life.

ADVENTESE

Familiar Acronyms

- **ABC:** Adventist Book Center.
- **AFM:** Adventist Frontier Missions.
- **ADRA:** Adventist Development and Relief Agency.
- **ASI:** Adventist-laymen's Services and Industries.
- **AY:** Adventist Youth. (In some churches, AY meetings are held on Sabbath afternoons.)
- **GC:** General Conference of Seventh-day Adventists.
- **NAD:** North American Division of Seventh-day Adventists.

---

* Dietrich Bonhoeffer, *The Cost of Discipleship* (Norwich, England: SCM Press, 2001), p. 17.
† Frederick Buechner, *Wishful Thinking: A Theological ABC* (New York: Harper & Row, 1973), p. 95.

Friday

CHECKING UP

For the following two questions, circle all the correct answers that apply.

1. In the beginning, what responsibilities and privileges did God give to Adam and Eve?
   A. Rule over all animals and living creatures.
   B. Tend the plants.
   C. Build a house.
   D. Talk face to face with God.

2. According to Jesus, what often keeps people from following Him?
   A. They don't really know Him.
   B. They put family relationships above their relationship with Him.
   C. They trust in their wealth more than in Him.
   D. They are sinners.

Examine Your Own Experience

Since you have begun or renewed your walk with Jesus, have you been making changes in your priorities? In the list below, check any priority that you are changing or thinking about changing.
____ How I manage my money.
____ The people I choose to associate with.
____ Whether I should change jobs or change the way I do my current job.
____ How much time I spend on media (Internet, TV, movies, etc.).

Extend Your Learning

What does your use of time tell you about your priorities? This next week keep track of the time you spend on all your activities. Use categories and record by blocks of time. For example, you may have such categories as eating, sleeping, time with children, time with spouse, social time with others, work, household chores, devotions, exercise, Internet, TV, travel, etc. When the week is completed, reflect on what the time chart tells you about your priorities.

More resources on this topic can be found at http://www.InStepWithJesus.org/Journey.

What Should I Do With My Life?

What is the most important question a human being must answer? It may be *What should I do with my life?* Embedded within that question are many others that must be answered along the way. How should I respond to Jesus? Should I marry? If so, whom? What vocation or career should I choose?

The question is not always completely answered in a person's youth. It often reappears in one's forties and is sometimes referred to as "midlife crisis" when one realizes in an existential way that half of life is over. Even then the question does not disappear but returns with a slightly different twist at the time of retirement: *What should I do with the rest of my life?*

New believers also face the question, *What should I do with my life?* when they meet Jesus and begin to follow Him. The new birth brings with it new goals, new values, and a new perspective on life. As a new believer, you may want guidance in how to deal with this most important of questions.

A few years ago, Po Bronson set out to interview people who had made changes in their careers after having studied for or worked in some other occupation. Although he wrote a book from a secular perspective, the concept of "calling" or vocation was powerful in many of the more than 50 personal stories he told.* What he learned about how people discovered their calling illustrates how God often reveals our calling to us—what we should do with our life.

There is no official list of noble careers. For the Christian, any kind of honest work can become a calling when it is engaged in as a ministry.

People think that their calling will just come clearly to them one day. But that is not usually how it works. For most people, their calling developed slowly over time.

Your interests and the experiences you have already had can provide a place for you to begin to look.

If you have lost a job because of your observance of Sabbath or some other commitment to Christ, you can take courage in the faithfulness of God to provide, and you may discover that your challenges may lead you to something more meaningful.

Bronson explains what gives people courage to make changes in their life. "I learned that it was in hard times that people usually changed the course of their life; in good times, they frequently only talked about change. Hard times forced them to overcome the doubts that normally gave them pause. It surprised me how often we hold ourselves back until we have no choice. So the people herein suffered layoffs, bankruptcies, divorces, evictions, illnesses, and the deaths of loved ones, and as a result they were as likely to stumble into a better life as they were to arrive there by reasoned planning."†

---

* Po Bronson, *What Should I Do With My Life: The True Story of People Who Answered the Ultimate Question* (New York: Random House, 2002).

† Ibid., p. xv.

LIFE AS A NEW DISCIPLE

Key Texts: *Matthew 3:13–17; 4:1–11; Mark 5:1–20; Luke 5:32; 19:1–9; Acts 19:23–41*

How can I cope with the major changes in my life that come from my discipleship?

What do these changes mean with regards to telling my friends about Jesus?

Now that I'm a disciple, will all of life's problems go away?

This week's memory text: " 'Go home to your friends, and tell them what great things the Lord has done for you, and how He has had compassion on you' " (Mark 5:19, NKJV).

Beginning a journey with Jesus is an emotion-filled experience. Like physical birth, spiritual rebirth brings both pain and great joy. There is the pain of the old self dying, which often results in losses of familiar routines, in altered family relationships, and maybe in occupational crises. Then there is the joy of the new self in Christ with its sense of forgiveness and peace with God, its new purposes in life, its desire to live more fully, its change in perspective that sees all things through the lens of God's Word. In this week's lesson we'll face reality as we look at changes that Jesus brought into the lives of people when He walked this earth.

Walking With Jesus in the Real World
Finding Jesus at a Class Reunion—*Carolyn Wilson**

I didn't have any problem with the doctrines; I just drifted out of the church. I didn't know Jesus personally. Both my husband and I were members of an Adventist church when we married. He had two sons by a previous marriage, and together we eventually had two daughters.

We owned and operated two businesses: a dune buggy store and a video rental service. Both were open seven days a week. Our life was work, work, work. Our daughters would spend the weekend with my mother, who took them to Sabbath School. The girls often begged me to go with them. Once I did, and my husband actually wrote me a note and said that I had to choose between going to church or working with him. For 22 years we lived in an Adventist community but not as Adventists.

Then the Adventist high school I had attended during my junior and senior years held its homecoming, and our class was the 25-year honor class. Although I had lost contact with most of my former classmates, at our homecoming reunion, I felt very included. Our class met together privately and people just bared their souls. The Holy Spirit had prepared me for this time because my own life had not been fulfilling. I met Jesus that weekend. God's love for me became so real.

A friend invited me to attend her Sabbath School class. Soon I bought a very nice Bible. I took it home and sat at the table turning the pages one by one to separate the gold edging. I became very emotional thinking that I was going to be studying the Word of God.

My husband saw how much I was changing and how happy I was. In three or four weeks, he, too, began to attend Sabbath School. And that's when our problems began. When he started coming to church, we had to close our businesses. We would open the store a half hour after sundown on Saturday. People would be lined up at the door, waiting to get in. At the time, our video business was the only one in the area, and we had a huge selection of videos of all ratings.

Soon we decided that we could no longer offer X-rated movies for rent. We burned them all. Then we began to wonder about the R-rated movies. My husband wanted to burn them, too, but I thought we should sell them to get some of our money back. We took them off the shelf, but did nothing with them.

About this time the Sabbath School lesson was on the book of Acts. When we read that new Christians had publicly burned their scrolls on sorcery, we knew what we had to do. We burned the R-rated videos also—altogether a $100,000 inventory.

Business was dropping off. People were angry. We no longer had the wide selection of videos, and we were closed on Sabbath. Our daughter, who worked for us, left to work for another video rental store. But this time, we never wavered. After a few months, we closed our video business.

---

* A pseudonym.

Monday

SURPRISING EXPERIENCES

A person's baptism is one of those high points in life when he or she later can remember the event in vivid detail and, perhaps, even the specific date. If you have recently been baptized or are looking forward to baptism or have renewed your baptismal vows, you may be experiencing the joy of a new relationship with Jesus.

This is the new birth. You see the world and your own life through new lenses. Jesus is giving you a new life, and even though you are an "infant" in that new life, you have faith and hope for what the future holds.

This scenario, however, may not reflect all that you are going through. What if it seems to you that troubles and temptations have increased since you committed your life to Jesus? Was your commitment not sincere? Is Jesus not faithful? Jesus' experience of His own baptism has some surprising elements. Read Matthew 3:13–17. What powerful affirmation of God's approval did Jesus receive at the time of His baptism?

This high experience at the time of Jesus' baptism surely remained a vivid memory for Him throughout His entire life. But this high point did not spare Him from temptation or troubles. Notice what happened right after His baptism; Mark says "immediately" (1:12). Read Matthew 4:1–11.

• What motivated Jesus to go to the wilderness? Read verse 1.

• What identical wording does the devil use in the first two temptations? Read verses 3, 6.

These words were intended to create doubt in Jesus' mind regarding His own identity and therefore, His own mission. Notice the title that the devil wants to undermine. At the time of Jesus' baptism, what title had the Voice from heaven given to Jesus? Read Matthew 3:17.

For Jesus to have accepted the devil's challenge would have been to doubt God's words. Are the temptations and troubles you are experiencing designed to cause you to doubt God's words or your commitment to Him?

After 40 days of fasting, Jesus was tempted to work independently from His Father to provide food for Himself, evidence that God would take care of Him, and all the power and possessions the world had to offer. But He did not give in. What method did Jesus use to deal with temptation? Read verses 4, 7, 10.

• What would you have to do to make that method available to yourself?

For more information on the temptation of Jesus, see "A Closer Look" on page 57.

Tuesday

MEETING JESUS CHANGES PEOPLE

It is no wonder the story of Zacchaeus is a favorite children's story. Zacchaeus was a short man who had trouble seeing over a crowd of people, but he solved his problem in a clever way. Children can relate to his shortness; for adults the story contains profound insights into how meeting Jesus changes a life. Read Luke 19:1–9. What did Zacchaeus want?

We know because of subsequent events that Zacchaeus's desire was not simply curiosity; he was asking the first basic question of a disciple: Who are You, Jesus? After he had met Jesus and given a dinner for Him, Zacchaeus answered the second question: What do You want me to do? Even though there is no record of Jesus lecturing him, what major commitments did Zacchaeus make?

1.

2.

• What emotions seem to be contained in his announcement? Read verse 8.

• How did Jesus feel? Read verses 9, 10.

Another little story about a man whom Jesus called to be a disciple shows how a person reacts when he or she first becomes a follower of Jesus. Read about Levi in Luke 5:27–31. What did he do to honor Jesus?

• Whom did he invite to this event?

The scribes and **Pharisees** did not approve of the guest list. In today's culture the terms "**tax collectors**" and "sinners" do not carry all of the negative connotations that they did in Jesus' day. Jesus, of course, squelched their criticism with what statement? Read Luke 5:32.

In one of these stories, we see a man making major changes in his life, including the correcting of past wrongs—all because he met Jesus. In the stories of Zacchaeus and Levi, the men's contact with Jesus led them to prepare a meal and joyfully introduce their friends to Him.

KEY TERMS

Pharisees—A conservative religious party that stressed separation from the world and its defilements.

Tax collectors—Also known as publicans, these people were especially hated because they worked for Rome and often demanded unreasonable payments.

CHANGING MASTERS

Whenever people come to Jesus with open minds and hearts, they are changed. One of the most dramatic stories of change occurred in **Gentile** territory in a remote area among the towns of the **Decapolis**. It is in Mark 5:1–20. Read the story twice and the second time you read it, try to visualize the events.

The man in this story is possessed by an "unclean spirit" (the NIV says "evil spirit"). The unclean spirit itself says there are many spirits living in the man. How completely was this man under the control of this spirit or spirits?

How complete was this man's healing—how different were his thoughts and behavior? Read verses 14, 15.

• What was the remarkable reaction of the people who lived in that area? Read verse 15.

• The people placed something over the value of human life. What evidence is there that people today have the same priorities?

• When Jesus got into the boat to leave, the formerly demon-possessed man begged to go with Him. What was Jesus' surprising response? Read verse 19.

• In what sense did the man follow Jesus after all?

ADVENTESE

Key historical figures

• **J. N. Andrews** (1829–1883): Scholar, writer; in 1874, sent to Switzerland as the first Adventist missionary to a country outside North America.

• **Joseph Bates** (1792–1872): Sea captain, preacher, one of the principal founders of the Seventh-day Adventist Church.

• **Uriah Smith** (1832–1903): At the age of 23 became editor of the *Review and Herald* (now *Adventist Review*); best known for his book, *Daniel and the Revelation*.

• **Ellen G. White** (1827–1915): Cofounder of the Seventh-day Adventist Church; writer, lecturer, and counselor to the church, who possessed what Adventists have accepted as the gift of prophecy as described in the Bible.

• **James White** (1821–1881): Founder of the Seventh-day Adventist Church and husband of Ellen White; founder and first editor of *The Present Truth, Review and Herald, Signs of the Times,* and *The Youth's Instructor*.

KEY TERMS

Gentiles—In New Testament times, any people who were not Jewish.

Decapolis—A league of ten cities that were centers of Greek and Roman culture; all but one were located east of the Sea of Galilee and the Jordan River.

THE POWER OF ECONOMICS

Even today many knowledgeable non-Christians are willing to say that Jesus was a great moral teacher. Why is it then, that the preaching of the gospel of Jesus often creates opposition? An example from the experiences of Paul as he went about Asia preaching may help explain in part. Read twice about an incident that occurred in Ephesus in Acts 19:23–41. Who was Demetrius?

What threat did Paul's preaching create for Demetrius and his fellow artisans?

The solution that Demetrius attempted was to incite a riot and run the evangelists out of town. If he had gone to the people and told them that his income (and the income of the other silversmiths who had joined with him) was threatened, people might have only yawned and said, "I'm sorry to hear that." But Demetrius cleverly expanded the threat to involve all the people. What was his convincing argument? Read verses 26, 27.

When Demetrius combined economic concerns with issues of public safety, it created a force powerful enough to incite a riot. What effect did this have on the work of Paul and his companions?

• What was the writer's assessment of the rioters? Read verse 32.

The disciples would not let Paul go before the assembly to try to quiet things because they feared for his life. They urged Alexander to make a defense, but with interesting results. Finally, help came from an unexpected source. Read verses 35–40. Who quieted the crowd?

• What was his convincing argument?

A CLOSER LOOK

The Temptation of Jesus

Contrary to what might be expected, strong temptations to doubt and disobey often come right after conversion or some other significant spiritual event. Jesus' temptations came right after His baptism, anointing by the Holy Spirit, and His Father saying, "This is My beloved Son."

Jesus did not wander into temptation; He was led to the wilderness by the Spirit. At His physically weakest moment—after 40 days of fasting—Satan came to tempt Him. Satan insinuated distrust: Would God really treat His Son like this? So Satan tempted Jesus to (1) put His physical needs above His spiritual needs; (2) use His supernatural power to challenge God, that is, to use His gifts for His own benefit; and (3) gain power and authority without enduring the Cross. Each temptation was an appeal to doubt God and reject His priorities.

Jesus found strength in the Word. Read Psalm 119:11.

CHECKING UP

Circle all that apply.

1. Once a person is baptized, what can he or she expect life to be like?
   A. No more money problems.
   B. No more relationship problems.
   C. Troubles and temptations continue.
   D. Increasing victories over sin as he or she depends on Jesus.

2. In this week's lesson, we studied three men who expressed their joy and gratitude to Jesus in tangible ways. Match the person to his action.

A. Demon-possessed man

B. Zacchaeus

C. Levi

_____ 1. Said he would repay four times the amount that he had cheated people.
_____ 2. Went around telling everyone what Jesus had done for him.
_____ 3. Gave a banquet in Jesus' honor.
_____ 4. Put clothes on.
_____ 5. Vowed to give half his money to the poor.
_____ 6. Begged to follow Jesus.

Examine Your Own Experience

The Christian life is often filled with paradoxes. Are you experiencing any of the following?
   A. Happiness with your new healthful lifestyle / disappointment in how frequently you are tempted with harmful behaviors
   B. Peace with your new relationship with Jesus / insecurity over your changing relationships with some family and friends
   C. Joy with the Sabbath / puzzlement over how to "keep the Sabbath"

Write your own personal paradox:

Extend Your Learning

Following in the footsteps of the people in this lesson, what can you do next week to express in a tangible way your gratitude and joy to Jesus for what He has done and is doing for you?

More resources on this topic can be found at http://www.InStepWithJesus.org/Journey.

Living a New History

Do you ever wish you could rewrite your own life story? Erase a childhood trauma? Change some decisions you made as a teenager? What you are today is an accumulation of all the days and experiences of your past. Would you like a new history?

Or maybe you are rather proud of your past and satisfied with who you are today. At one point in his life, Paul was quite proud of who he was. He followed all of the religious traditions; he was a "Hebrew of Hebrews"; he kept the letter of the law and was so zealous for it that he persecuted those who did not (Phil. 3:4–6). But when he met the risen Christ on the road to Damascus, he gained a new insight into who Christ really was.

Whether your old history is one you are ashamed of or one you are smugly proud of, you must walk away from it before you can become a child of God through Jesus Christ. Paul said he counted his past as "rubbish" so that he could have life (righteousness) from Christ and not from his own goodness (by working hard at obeying the law) (verse 8). Paul needed a new history.

How is it possible to get rid of an old history and gain a new history? You get rid of your old history by dying to it. "No other way exists to break the power of the past."* The great Christian symbol of baptism lets you act out your death by uniting to Jesus' death, and just as Jesus was raised from the dead to life, you, too, as you come out of the water, are raised to a new life, a new history (Rom. 6:3–7). In an amazing gift of God, Jesus' history of a perfect life becomes your history. So you no longer have to be a slave to sin. There is power in the resurrection of Jesus.

"If you are under grace, you have a new history in Jesus Christ. At the ultimate center of everything that matters, you are accepted—you are OK—regardless of where you have been or what you have done. God's grace and acceptance become a mighty work in you that lifts you up and gives you a fresh start every day. Not because you deserve it, but because God, in His grace, provided it for you in Jesus Christ. It is a divine act just as mighty as the Exodus. . . . When you make mistakes, when the old history rears up its head inside, you can 'count yourself' once again dead to sin and alive in Christ. If a part of your body reaches out to do the wrong thing, you can offer that part of your body to God each day. Sin will not be your master when you are living in God's grace daily. Although you continue to have daily battles to fight, the new history overcomes the old history."†

* Jon Paulien, *Meet God Again for the First Time* (Hagerstown, Md.: Review and Herald®, 2003), p. 121.
† Ibid., p. 123.

LESSON 8

JESUS' PATIENCE WITH HIS DISCIPLES

Key Texts: *Matthew 14:22, 23; 18:21, 22; 26:69–75; Mark 1:16, 17; 14:27–31; 16:7; John 13:1–17; 21:1–14, 19; Acts 1:15–26; 2:14–41; 1 Peter 5:2*

Can I still be a disciple of Jesus even after I have sinned?
Do the stories of Peter's failures have relevance for me?
How long will it take until I finally get my life in order?

This week's memory text: " 'Go, tell His disciples—and Peter—that He is going before you into Galilee; there you will see Him, as He said to you' " (Mark 16:7, NKJV).

Sunday

Of the twelve disciples of Jesus, we are told the most about Peter. As a high-energy person, he often served as a spokesman and a representative of the other disciples. During his time with Jesus, he went from high points of faith to the lowest of betrayal. Although Jesus rebuked Peter severely on one occasion, He continued to teach him throughout the three years of His time with the disciples and finally compassionately forgave Peter for his great sin and entrusted him with a great mission. In many ways, the story of Peter is the story of every disciple. And the patience that Jesus had with Peter, He extends to all of us.

Walking With Jesus in the Real World

A long and difficult struggle—*Jake Caldwell**

It was baseball at first. I was hitting home runs right from the start. Then one of my friends gave me an old lacrosse stick, and I got into that sport the next season. It all developed from there: ice hockey, basketball, football, ping pong, tennis, and golf. I played them all. A football injury ended my career before it ever got off the ground. I wound up in a depression that hardly lifted for ten years.

I jumped around from one job to another: sparring partner for a champion Canadian kickboxer, then boxing, floor manager of a bar, and dance trainer. But I was not happy. Once I got into a bar fight and broke a man's face.

Eventually, working in a welding shop owned by two Adventists and logging for them in the winter, I was brought to Christ. An evangelistic series made a believer out of me. I was delivered from a tobacco addiction, stopped drinking, and started to study the Bible with the local pastor.

I was starting a new journey in life, but the trouble was not over. I was depressed and lonely. My lack of tact made it difficult for others to feel at ease around me. At times I even scared people with a look of intimidation. Violence was second nature to me.

I was hopeful but confused after baptism. I began to study the Bible and the writings of E. G. White. They brought hope and joy but much self-condemnation.

I met an Adventist girl, and we married. I can truly say that except for the grace of God my marriage would have failed in the first month. Jesus was trying to teach me to give up on my old self and to let God live His life through mine.

It has been a long and difficult struggle, but I found the shortcut about seven years ago.

I read the book *Practicing the Presence of God.* The author loved to be in the presence of God. He was still self-hating at times, even of a lazy nature, yet he did everything in the presence of a loving Father as unto the Lord, and this intrigued me.

Later I started to study the Bible and the Spirit of Prophecy with a different focus. I was beginning to challenge myself to see God as One who could love even me, just as I was, and for the purpose of changing my heart. This helped my marriage and other relationships also.

After working as a construction subcontractor for six years, I started my own company installing siding and doing renovations. My wife and I have partnered with God. We pay a double tithe, have less than one year left on our mortgage, and give to the poor systematically.

I love to share the things of God, my Savior and my Friend.

I am not yet the meekest man that ever walked the earth, like Moses. But I am growing in grace and in favor both with God and with men.

The sins of my youth still are ever before me, yet I know the love of God like never before. Jesus has become my Rock and my hiding Place. I fully embrace His love and know only Christ and Him crucified as my staple spiritual food.

---

* A pseudonym.

Monday

TEACHING AND RESCUING ALONG THE WAY

Jesus often taught His disciples lessons that came from their life together. Peter provided many opportunities for Jesus to correct faulty or incomplete understanding or to rescue him from himself. In an earlier lesson, we learned how Jesus used a severe rebuke to correct Peter's misunderstanding of the role of the Messiah. Today we will see how Jesus related to Peter in three other incidents.

Jesus had just miraculously fed 5,000 men plus women and children. The people were so excited that they were planning to take Jesus by force and make Him king (John 6:15). How did Jesus deal with this volatile situation? Read Matthew 14:22, 23.

Read in verses 24–43 the rest of the story that continues into a stormy night on the Sea of Galilee. How did Peter demonstrate both faith and doubt?

• If you have ever experienced both faith and doubt, describe the experience.

On one occasion when Jesus was teaching the disciples a number of important lessons, He talked about how we should treat our fellow believers when they sin against us. When Jesus finished, Peter asked a question about forgiveness and received a shocking answer. Read Matthew 18:21, 22. Contrast the numbers involved.

Peter was being literal with his number and quite generous. Many rabbis of that day said that a person is obligated to forgive only three times. In the large number that Jesus gave, what was He trying to teach Peter and the rest of us?

In John 13:1–17, read about the poignant scene in the **upper room** when Jesus was washing the disciples' feet. Why do you think Peter objected to having Jesus wash his feet?

Jesus said that Peter would not understand the significance of the footwashing until later. What did Peter need to learn about how he should relate to the actions and teachings of Jesus?

KEY TERMS

Upper room—The room where Jesus and His twelve disciples ate the Passover meal, that is, the **Last Supper**.
Last Supper—The last meal that Jesus and His disciples ate together before His arrest.

Tuesday
DISOWNING JESUS

For nearly three years Peter was privileged to travel with Jesus around the countryside and in the cities. He saw Jesus heal lepers, restore sight to the blind, raise Lazarus, and feed large numbers of people by multiplying a single lunch. He stood on the mountain with James and John when they witnessed the dazzling transfiguration of Jesus and heard the Voice from heaven say, " 'This is My beloved Son, in whom I am well pleased' " (Matt. 17:5, NKJV).

Time after time he had seen that Jesus did everything with His mission in mind, yet, at the end of their time together—right after the Last Supper, Peter once again doubted what Jesus told the disciples. Read Mark 14:27–31. What did Jesus say would happen before the night was over?

• How did Peter contradict Jesus' prediction?

The next scene with Peter occurs in the courtyard of the high priest. He had followed Jesus at a distance and was now waiting for the outcome of the trial that was underway. Read Matthew 26:69–75. Indicate how each denial gets more intense:

1.

2.

3.

• What was Peter's reaction when he heard the rooster crow?

Only hours earlier Peter had vowed to die before he would deny Jesus, yet he denied Him not because he was faced with death, but because a servant girl said that he had been with Jesus in Galilee. What was Peter's problem?

• Why did he so readily deny his Master?

Consider this: In what ways might we be like Peter?

Wednesday

RESTORATION

After the crucifixion and resurrection of Jesus, He appeared occasionally to the disciples during a 40-day period. On one of the last occasions, the disciples had been fishing unsuccessfully all night, and in the morning as they approached shore, they met Jesus, though they did not recognize Him at first. Read John 21:1–14.

After Jesus gave them breakfast, He took Peter aside and engaged him in a crucially important dialogue. Read verses 15–19. Of what would the three repeated questions, "Do you love Me?" have reminded Peter?

• Notice how Peter's responses differed. How did he respond to the first question?

• How did he respond to the third question?

• By the time that Jesus asked that third time, what was Peter thinking or feeling?

By His persistent probing, Jesus opened Peter's wounded heart and forced him to confront his own weakness. Each time Peter confessed his love for Jesus, Jesus told him, respectively: "Feed My lambs," "Feed My sheep," "Feed My sheep." In this incident, what is linked with love for Jesus?

When Peter wrote his **epistle** to Christians scattered across Asia Minor, he included instructions to leaders of the church. What wording suggests that throughout his life Peter carried in his mind Jesus' conversation with him after the Resurrection? Read 1 Peter 5:2.

Compare the final instruction that Jesus gave Peter at this last meeting with the instruction He gave Peter the first time He met him. Read John 21:19; Mark 1:16, 17. What does this tell us about the role of a disciple?

ADVENTESE

Common Expressions

• **Lay activity:** Christian witnessing to others by nonclergy; sometimes "lay activity," spoken with tongue-in-cheek, means a Sabbath afternoon nap.

• **Like the leaves of autumn:** An expression to describe the way in which small tracts and pamphlets are widely distributed.

• **My favorite author:** An oblique way of referring to Ellen White.

• **Received a call:** Was offered a job in church denominational work.

• **Right arm of the message:** Medical work or teaching healthful living.

• **Servant of the Lord:** Another way of referring to Ellen White.

• **Spirit of Prophecy says:** Ellen White says . . .

KEY TERMS

Epistle—A letter written by an apostle with instruction for one or more churches.

THE POWER OF ECONOMICS

After Peter's confession and repentance and his assurance of being forgiven by Jesus, he was ready to serve his Lord. His name appears first in the list of disciples given after Jesus' ascension. And he is the one who led out in choosing a disciple to replace Judas. Read Acts 1:15–26.

After the Holy Spirit was poured out on the believers at **Pentecost**, Peter gave the first of the "missionary addresses" recorded in the book of Acts. He began by explaining why the disciples were speaking in languages understood by travelers from many countries. Who stood with Peter as he began his sermon? Read Acts 2:14.

These were the men who had seen and could testify to the risen Christ. Read in Acts 2:14–41 the entire presentation given by a transformed and Holy Spirit-empowered disciple. What was the result of Peter's preaching?

Were Peter's days of learning from Jesus over? Even though Jesus was not physically present with Peter, He still had lessons to teach him. Through Peter Jesus taught the early church a lesson that was essential for taking the gospel to the entire world. The story begins in Acts 10:1–8 with a Roman officer. What was the officer told to do?

The scene now turns to Peter, who was on a roof praying. What strange vision did he receive? Read Acts 10:9–16.

• What was the meaning of the vision? Read verses 17–48.

This lesson that Peter learned experientially was so important for the young church that Luke told it twice. Read Acts 11; 15:6–9. What barriers did the lesson break down?

A CLOSER LOOK

Jesus' Patience With Peter

All the disciples deserted Jesus at His arrest. Later Peter even denied that he knew Him. Yet Jesus did not reject them. After His resurrection, an angel told the women who came to the empty tomb, " 'Go, tell His disciples—and Peter—that He is going before you into Galilee; there you will see Him, as He said to you' " (Mark 16:7, NKJV).

Jesus had not removed the deserters from their roles as His disciples. By mentioning Peter by name, Peter knew that Jesus had accepted his repentance and had forgiven him. Later at an early morning breakfast by the sea and in front of all the disciples, "Jesus revealed the depth of Peter's repentance, and showed how thoroughly humbled was the once boasting disciple.'"

KEY TERMS

Pentecost—The fiftieth day after the Sabbath of Passover week. The day the Holy Spirit descended on the disciples.

---

* *The Desire of Ages,* p. 812.

Friday

CHECKING UP

Match the incident involving Peter or one of his statements to the lesson that Jesus taught him.

Incident or statement	Lesson learned

___ 1. Offering to forgive seven times.

___ 2. "I will not deny you."

___ 3. Believed that God does not accept Gentiles.

___ 4. Jesus washing his feet.

___ 5. Walking on water.

___ 6. "I don't know the man."

A. Keep focused on Jesus.

B. God will pour out His Spirit on anyone who believes in Him.

C. Believers should always extend grace to those in need.

D. We need to recognize our real selves.

E. Trust Jesus' actions even when we don't understand.

F. Be faithful to Jesus even in difficult situations.

Examine Your Own Experience

Read carefully the list of lessons that Peter learned. Of those lessons, identify two that you think you are most in need of learning.

1.

2.

Extend Your Learning

Peter wrote two epistles to fellow believers. His second epistle was written near the end of his life and is considered his last testament. Read the section that gives evidence that Peter is writing near the end of his life and consider the event that he singles out as one evidence of the power and majesty of Jesus. Read 2 Peter 1:12–18.

More resources on this topic can be found at http://www.InStepWithJesus.org/Journey.

The Famous Twelve Steps

A meeting in Akron, Ohio, in 1935, between Bill W., a New York stockbroker, and Dr. Bob S., an Akron surgeon, saved the life of one of them and resulted in the saving of thousands of other lives. Both men had been hopeless alcoholics. Dr. Bob was still an alcoholic. But Bill, under the spiritual influence of the noted Episcopalian clergyman, Dr. Samuel Shoemaker, and with the help of an old-time friend, had gotten sober.

Dr. Bob had tried unsuccessfully to get sober but had failed. When he came face-to-face with Bill, a fellow sufferer who had made good, the effect on him was profound. "Bill emphasized that alcoholism was a malady of mind, emotions, and body."* With this new insight, Dr. Bob soon got sober and never drank again.

Together the men began to work with alcoholics at Akron's City Hospital, "where one patient quickly achieved sobriety."† These three men formed the nucleus of the first Alcoholics Anonymous group. Early in 1939, they published *Alcoholics Anonymous.* Written by Bill, the text explains AA's philosophy and methods, the core of which was the now well-known "Twelve Steps of Recovery."

These are the original Twelve Steps.
1. We admitted we were powerless over alcohol—that our lives had become unmanageable.
2. Came to believe that a Power greater than ourselves could restore us to sanity.
3. Made a decision to turn our will and our lives over to the care of God as we understood Him.
4. Made a searching and fearless moral inventory of ourselves.
5. Admitted to God, to ourselves, and to another human being the exact nature of our wrongs.
6. We're entirely ready to have God remove all these defects of character.
7. Humbly asked Him to remove our shortcomings.
8. Made a list of all persons we had harmed, and became willing to make amends to them all.
9. Made direct amends to such people wherever possible, except when to do so would injure them or others.
10. Continued to take personal inventory and when we were wrong promptly admitted it.
11. Sought through prayer and meditation to improve our conscious contact with God as we understood Him, praying only for knowledge of His will for us and the power to carry that out.
12. Having had a spiritual awakening as the result of these steps, we tried to carry this message to alcoholics, and to practice these principles in all our affairs.

Today other problems, in addition to alcoholism, are recognized as addictions. The 12-Step program has been adapted to deal with many of these. Christians have adapted the 12 steps to deal with the "addiction" of sin in whatever form it manifests itself.

Regeneration Ministry, a part of the Health Ministries Department of the North American Division of Seventh-day Adventists, has developed a 12-step program titled "Journey to Wholeness." This program leads participants to the power of God for overcoming sinful behaviors.

---

* "Historical Data: The Birth of A.A. and Its Growth in U.S./Canada," retrieved November 13, 2009, www.aa.org/lang/en/subpage .cfm?page=288.
† Ibid.

THE BIBLE AS A GUIDE FOR LIFE

Key Texts: *Psalm 119:105; Matthew 4:1–11; 5:17, 18; 22:23–40; Luke 2:41–52; 4:14–21; John 7:14, 15; 8:12; Acts 2:14–41; 1 John 2:3–6; Revelation 1:12–18*

Since the Bible was written thousands of years ago, how can it be a guide for my life today?

Is there any help in the Bible for the issues I face today?

Do I need a college education to understand the Bible?

This week's memory text: *"Your word is a lamp to my feet and a light to my path"* (Ps. 119:105, NKJV).

As a new or returning follower of Jesus, you understand that the Bible has become or should become a very important Book in your life. In fact, in the Bible you will find your values, your purpose in life, and how to follow Jesus. But there is one small problem between your desire to use the Bible as a guide for your life and your ability to do so: the Bible is no ordinary Book. In fact, it is composed of 66 books, written across a span of 1,500 years, and the last book was written just over 2,000 years ago. Furthermore, the geographic and the cultural setting for all the books of the Bible are far removed from your life today. How can these gaps be bridged? We will explore the process this week.

Walking With Jesus in the Real World

Changing Careers—*David Browning**

I had just returned home from college for the summer when I received a phone call from Montreal. The person on the line offered me a position as a police officer with the Royal Canadian Mounted Police (RCMP). I was ecstatic! It was a dream come true.

Two years earlier I had applied to be trained as an officer in the RCMP and then had gone through extensive testing, interviews, and a security check. Now, having been accepted, I entered the police academy. On the day of my graduation, I was 22 years old, making a good salary, and had a badge in my pocket.

I had given my heart to Jesus in my teens but had drifted away. I still considered myself a Christian but was not living the Christian life.

In the process of tracking down witnesses and suspects one day, I met a family that owned horses. Because of my love of horses, I often returned to their home. Another draw to the family was their attractive daughter Marti, who, in time, became my wife.

When our first child was born, we wanted to take him to church, but which church? Marti had grown up in an Adventist home, but my family's church background was of a different denomination. I thought going to church on Saturday was ridiculous. After going to pastors from both churches with my questions, I began to study with the Adventist pastor. A short time after settling some questions about the Sabbath and other doctrines and Ellen White, both Marti and I were baptized into the Seventh-day Adventist Church.

That important day led to my resignation from the RCMP and my entrance into Canadian University College, an Adventist instution, to study for the ministry.

In my pastoral ministry, I tried to become involved as a police chaplain. The door never did open. Then I had an opportunity to become an auxiliary member, a volunteer cop with the RCMP. I thought this would satisfy my law enforcement interests, but as soon as I started volunteering, I knew I had to get back into it full time.

I did return to the RCMP. When I returned, church people asked me how I could leave the ministry. I told them I haven't left the ministry. I have just remodeled my pulpit. It used to be made of wood or Plexiglas. Now it is made out of asphalt, rubber, and steel.

I am now called upon to meet the needs of the people at a street level, whether it is to arrest the burglar who just entered their home or to stop the teenage speeder from killing himself. I am called to minister by breaking up a fight that could lead to injury or death and by notifying a mother that her son is dead. I go places a pastor could never go. But I haven't left the ministry. I still get to preach. From time to time, it is behind a pulpit, but mostly it is by helping others in their time of need.

---

* A pseudonym.

Monday

DISCIPLES AND THE BIBLE

Learning to be a Christian and learning to be a disciple are the same thing. Christians are disciples of Jesus. Jesus Himself told us what is involved in being one of His disciples. See Luke 9:23, 24. He said we must follow Him. To follow Him, we have to know Him. The disciple/apostle John explains how we can tell if we know Jesus and if we are abiding in Him. Read 1 John 2:3–6.

• What is the evidence that we know Jesus?

• What is the evidence that we abide in Him?

   Our only source for knowing Jesus and His teachings is the Bible as it is brought to life for us by the Holy Spirit. Jesus is the central Character in the Bible. He is central in the New Testament, which was written after His life on earth, but also in the Old Testament, which was written years before He was born to Mary. The Old Testament contains the promise; the New Testament contains the fulfillment. The first book in the Bible gives a hint—a promise in embryo form—of the Savior that was to come. Read Genesis 3:15.

• To whom was God speaking?

• Who will have his head bruised?

• Who will have His heel bruised?

   In the very last book of the Bible, John describes the glorified Christ whom he saw in vision. Read the description in Revelation 1:12–18. What aspect of the description impresses you most?

   From beginning to end, the Bible is the story of how God interacts with human beings. And that is the story of Jesus Christ.

   In the Gospels we see Jesus teaching His disciples. In the rest of the New Testament, we learn how the disciples functioned after Jesus' resurrection when He was no longer physically with them. We have glimpses of the importance of Scripture to them. Of course, the only Scripture they had was the Old Testament. Three of the Twelve (Matthew, John, and Peter) wrote books in the New Testament. Whenever the disciples spoke or wrote to a Jewish audience who would know the Scriptures, they quoted from these three authors. They used the Scriptures as an authoritative source.

   Open your Bible and just glance through these chapters and verses. If your Bible indicates Old Testament quotations by Italics or indentation, you will see the disciples' familiarity with the Scriptures. Read Acts 2:14–41; Matthew 1–3; and all of 2 Peter. Disciples today should also use the Scriptures as their authority and guide.

HOW JESUS USED SCRIPTURE

The Gospel records of the life of Jesus are silent about the years between His toddler years (return from **exile in Egypt**) and the time His parents lost Him for a short time at the age of 12 only to find Him in the temple, listening to the scholarly teachers and asking questions. It can surely be inferred that their topic of conversation dealt with Scripture and that Jesus knew a lot about it. Read Luke 2:41–52. In the great temptation scenes with Satan, Jesus provides an example of how to deal with temptation. Read Matthew 4:1–11. What does Jesus use to combat temptation?

A question that confronts all of us is, What should I do with my life? Through communion with His Father and in the Scriptures, Jesus discovered His own mission in life. One day in His hometown, He stood up in the synagogue and announced His mission in life by reading from the book of Isaiah. Read Luke 4:14–21. Summarize what this passage, quoted from Isaiah, reveals about Jesus' mission.

In His teaching and in His interaction with others, Jesus often quoted Scripture. Although it is difficult to be precise, it is estimated that He quoted from more than 20 Old Testament books. He was thoroughly acquainted with the Scriptures. Read John 7:14, 15.

Obviously, Jesus had studied the Scriptures a great deal. What the people meant by this comment is that He had never formally studied with a Jewish teacher. It is still true that in our culture, it is not necessary to have a college education to learn the Scriptures.

A CLOSER LOOK

Why Memorize Scripture?

"There is nothing more calculated to strengthen the intellect than the study of the Scriptures. No other book is so potent to elevate the thoughts, to give vigor to the faculties, as the broad, ennobling truths of the Bible."[*]

As a disciple, you desire to be like Jesus, to walk as He walked. That takes transformation from your "old self" to a "new self." Paul urges you to "be transformed by the renewing of your mind" (Rom. 12:2, NKJV). Filling your mind with memorized Scripture assists with this renewal of mind.

The great Reformer Martin Luther had so much of the Bible memorized that when he first gained insight from Romans 1:17 into justification by faith, he said, "Thereupon I ran through the Scriptures from memory"[†] in order to confirm that insight.

KEY TERMS

Exile in Egypt—Being warned by an angel that Herod was seeking to kill the Infant Jesus, Joseph and Mary fled with Jesus to Egypt and stayed there until Herod died.

[*] *Steps to Christ,* p. 90.
[†] *Luther's Works,* 34:337.

Wednesday

HOW JESUS VALUED SCRIPTURE

By quoting a certain text in response to Satan's first temptation, Jesus made an important statement about the value of Scripture. Read the original Old Testament text and then Jesus' quotation of it in Deuteronomy 8:3 and Matthew 4:4. What principle does this text teach us regarding the value of Scripture?

Jesus valued the Scripture as a guide for human behavior. In a large section of the Sermon on the Mount, Jesus refers to Scripture and then expands on its meaning, showing that keeping the letter of the law was inadequate. He opened that section with a clear statement on the importance of Scripture. Read Matthew 5:17, 18. What did Jesus say was His relationship to the "**Law and the Prophets**"?

One day a group of **Sadducees** came to Jesus and challenged Him with an unusual situation. After listening to their story, Jesus said they had made two mistakes. What were those two mistakes? Read Matthew 22:23–33.

• Mistake 1:

• Mistake 2:

• In what way does Jesus' response place value on Scripture?

For a disciple, knowing Scripture is essential. Even the Old Testament, written before Jesus' time on earth, helps us to understand who He is and what His purpose is. After His crucifixion, but before the disciples knew He had arisen from the dead, He met two of them on the road to Emmaus, sadly discussing His death. Without revealing His true identity, He talked with them as they walked along, and they did not recognize Him. What was the content of His conversation? Read Luke 24:25–27.

That content certainly gives another indication of the value Jesus placed on Scripture.

KEY TERMS

Law and the Prophets—An expression used by people in Jesus' day to refer to all of the sacred Scriptures from what we know today as the Old Testament.

Sadducees—A minority religiopolitical Jewish party of New Testament times, representing the wealthy, aristocratic, liberal, secular-minded wing of Judaism.

Thursday
FINDING GUIDANCE

How can the Scriptures help you know and follow God's will? By now you know that there is no way you can look in an index or do an electronic search through the Bible to find direct answers to questions such as, Should I marry so-and-so? Should I stay in my current job or resign and prepare for a full-time ministry?

You may have heard of someone who wants to have a specific answer from God to a particular question, and so will ask the question, then open the Bible to a random place, lay a finger on the page, and then look to see what he or she thinks God has told him or her. This method is definitely not recommended. It has more in common with gambling than with finding the will of God. You can use a single text in such a way that it goes *against* the will of God.

Perhaps people turn to such questionable methods because more reliable ways are more difficult and more time consuming. To know God's will for your life, you need to be familiar with the Bible. You need to know what Jesus teaches. Some things are very plain. In fact, Jesus Himself summed up all the teachings of the Scriptures into two commands. What are those commands? Read Matthew 22:35–40. What are those two commands?

1.

2.

You can know that your decisions need to be made within the parameters of these two commands.

But what should you do if all of the options of a decision are within the parameters of these two commands? It is the consensus of many mature Christians that there are three things that work together to help a Christian make a decision within the will of God. These are the following:

• Passages of Scripture
• Impressions of the Holy Spirit
• Circumstances (including the counsel of other believers)

When all three of these indicators lead to the same conclusion, you can have more confidence that you will make the right decision. Sometimes others who have been walking with Jesus for a longer time can help you discern the will of God. Read a story about such mentoring in 1 Samuel 3:1–18. What impresses you most in this story?

Few of us hear God speak to us audibly, but we know that the Bible, as it is impressed on our minds by the Holy Spirit, is the Word of God to us. Becoming a Christian who wants to follow God's will does not mean that you must ignore your own judgment about the best course of action. And it does not mean that you will never make a wrong decision. According to Jesus, what advantage comes from following Him? Read John 8:12.

CHECKING UP

Circle all that apply.

1. What evidence do we have that Jesus studied the Scriptures of what we now call the Old Testament?
    A. Jesus quoted Scripture to resist temptation.
    B. He found His mission in life in the Scriptures.
    C. Matthew records that Jesus memorized all of the psalms.
    D. Jesus knew the Scriptures so well that He understood the principles that they teach.
    E. Jesus quoted from every Old Testament book.

2. What are the challenges of using the Bible as a guide in your own life?
    A. The books of the Bible were written a long time ago.
    B. Over centuries of copying the Scriptures by hand, serious errors go into the texts.
    C. I don't know much about what the Bible teaches.
    D. The Bible does not seem related to the decisions I must make.
    E. I don't spend much time studying the Bible.

Examine Your Own Experience

How do you make decisions? Do you make a list of all the pros and cons of each option? Do you consult with other people? Do you ask God for signs? Do you pray for guidance? Do you pray, open your Bible at a random place, put your finger on a text, and try to interpret how the text relates to your decision? Other ways? No matter what method or methods you use, how do you allow the Scriptures and the Holy Spirit to influence your decision?

Extend Your Learning

How can the Scriptures help you know and follow God's will? By now you know that there is no way you can look in an index or do an electronic search through the Bible to find direct answers to decisions you must make. To find information on using the Bible as a guide to life, go to this week's lesson helps at www .InStepWithJesus.org/Journey.

How Can I Know God's Will?

If you want to know God's will, you have to know how to recognize His voice. There are a lot of voices competing with His.

We are engulfed in communication chaos, but fortunately we cannot hear it or see it unless we choose to. Suppose you are walking along a trail in a park. Across the way you can see a lake sparkling from the reflection of the sun. Looking up you can see the blue sky and white clouds. You might hear children at play.

What you can't see or hear are the thousands of radio and television programs running through the atmosphere or the millions of cell phone messages and Internet searches traveling wirelessly all around you. How overbearing it would be if these things were visible and audible. Fortunately you can get these communications only if you have the right receiver: a radio, television set, cell phone, or computer. Without a receiver, you can't get the message.

A similar principle is at work when you seek to know God's will. You must be the kind of receiver that can recognize His voice. Jesus said, " 'The sheep follow him, for they know his voice' " (John 10:4, NKJV). You need to stay close to the Shepherd if you want to hear His voice.

God can use any means to speak to us. Indeed, He once used a donkey. (Read Numbers 22:28–30.) However, He usually reveals His will to us through His Written Word, through providential circumstances, and through impressions of the Holy Spirit.

Written Word. As we have learned, the Bible was written centuries ago and is composed of many forms of literature. You will find no specific guidance on most of the decisions you must make today. The Bible gives guidance through general principles and commands. If we disregard the clear commands of God, what point is there in seeking His will on some specific matter? For example, if a married man is having an affair with a coworker, isn't it presumptuous for him to ask God whether or not he should file for a divorce from his wife?

Providential circumstances. Unusual coincidences, a surprising incident, a series of events, the comment of a friend: all may be used by God to communicate with us. Providential circumstances are typically used as a confirmation of a choice you are already considering.

Impressions of the Holy Spirit. The Holy Spirit has direct access to our heart and mind. He can impress us with the course of action we should take. Unfortunately, our own fallen nature can also make known its desires. Telling the difference between impressions of the Holy Spirit and the desires of our own self is not easy. Sometimes other believers who know both God and us can help us discern the Holy Spirit's voice.

All three of these avenues of communication are interdependent. Waiting until all three are in harmony will give you the greatest assurance of God's will in a particular decision you must make.

LESSON 10

AUTHORITY OF THE BIBLE

Key Texts: *Numbers 12:6; Psalm 19:1–4; Luke 1:1–4; John 16:12, 13; 14:25, 26; Romans 1:20, 21; 1 Corinthians 2:13, 14; 2 Timothy 3:16, 17; Hebrews 4:12; 1 Peter 1:10–12; 2 Peter 1:21*

Why do we have a Bible?
How does the Bible differ from any other book?
How can I be confident that the Bible was inspired by God?
Are all the books of the Bible inspired?

This week's memory text: *"All Scripture is given by inspiration of God, and is profitable for doctrine, for reproof, for correction, for instruction in righteousness, that the man of God may be complete, thoroughly equipped for every good work"* (2 Tim. 3:16, 17, NKJV).

Perhaps the most basic question a person can ask is, Why is there something instead of nothing? Why are there oceans and land and trees and animals and human beings? Who or what brought them into existence?

Science can answer many questions about nature, but it cannot answer the question, Where does life come from? People throughout recorded history have answered that question by believing that life was given by some kind of supernatural god. But nature itself gives only secondary hints of what this God is like. We know only what God has chosen to reveal about Himself. And Christians believe that God does the revealing through both the created world and the Bible. This week we will consider the nature of the Bible itself and how we can have confidence in its divine authority.

Walking With Jesus in the Real World

Finding the Perfect Jesus

In her early twenties, Andrea left the church and began "living in the world." She did whatever she wanted to do and considered herself a decent person. In time she began to call herself an agnostic. "I thought there was a Higher Power, but no one could learn anything about it," she said.

Andrea eventually met Karl, who also had no interest in religion. He was a stable, normal person, not expressing any interest in moral issues. She remembers thinking, *See, he's happy. We can be happy without God or Jesus.* But she learned that life was more complex than merely seeking happiness.

A turning point came in Andrea's life when her first child was born. On the day of the birth, she was determined to remain unemotional. It was her nurse's training that made her want to be prepared for anything that might occur. But when her baby girl was placed in her arms and looked at her, an overwhelming sense of joy flooded over her. Her husband, who was in the delivery room, said, "When the baby came out, she was face up, and she looked dead. Her eyes were shut and she was not breathing. But in a second she began to breathe."

"I knew that it was God who had given her life," Andrea says. "This child who had been inside of me was alive all that time. The medical world has no explanation for that."

Over the next few weeks, she kept reliving the birth experience. "There has to be a God. It was too perfect. Too miraculous," she says. "God used that experience as a springboard for me to grow." In about a month, she called her father and said, "I want to go to church." So after about 15 years, she went back to the church where she had been baptized.

One Sabbath the person who was telling the children's story said to the children, "Did you notice that the little girl had pride? Jesus doesn't want us to have pride."

But Andrea thought, *Yes, He does want us to have a certain kind of pride.* She had absorbed the secular way of thinking and had many things to relearn from the Christian perspective. "It was like peeling an onion to remove the world from me. But the shedding went rapidly." For her it wasn't a burden; it was a joy.

Besides attending more than one Bible study a week, she kept *The Desire of Ages* at her bedside. The biggest treat of the day was getting to read that book before she went to bed. "It was like I was in love," she says. "When it was time to close the book, it wasn't enough." She marveled at the perfection of Jesus' nature and at His perfect words spoken at the perfect time. Although she had always sought happiness, she realized that what she really needed—but didn't know—was the love that Jesus gives.

"God sometimes reaches us through bad or tragic events," Andrea says. "But He reached me through a happy experience."

WHAT NATURE SAYS ABOUT GOD

With news reports constantly reminding us that nature itself is being threatened by human activity, many young adults are entering careers that try to restore an ecological balance to nature. We have all become more aware of the wonders that we find in nature, and when we climb in the mountains or cross a great river or see a film of the creatures that live in the ocean or see a newborn baby, we want to praise and worship the One who gave us these things. The psalmist David expresses our emotions in Psalm 19:1–4. What message did he get from nature?

• What does Paul say that nature tells us about God? Read Romans 1:20, 21.

• What effect does this knowledge have on humans if they do not honor Him?

What nature tells us about God has been labeled "general revelation." It tells us a few things in general about God, but it also sends a mixed message. First of all, there are the beauties and wonders of nature. But second, there are terrible, destructive forces in nature. Hurricanes, tornados, earthquakes, tsunamis, floods, droughts—all these things cause death and great suffering to human beings and other life on earth. Is the God who gives us beauty in nature the same God who gives us disaster in nature?

Nature itself is silent on this question. Only as the God of nature reveals Himself can we know His character and His will. To know God, we have to have a "special revelation" from Him. Christians believe that this special revelation comes in the Bible.

A CLOSER LOOK

Forming of the canon

The *canon* refers to the books that are included in the Bible and are accepted as inspired by God and, therefore, as possessing divine authority.

"No historical account of the formation of the Old Testament has been preserved, either in the Scriptures themselves or in other reliable historical documents."[*] Jesus' reference to "the Scriptures" and His use of them indicate that there was during His time a definite collection of writings that He considered to have divine authority.

The formation of the New Testament canon was a gradual process from the second to the fourth century. The 27 books of the New Testament, as we have them today, first appeared in A.D. 367 in an Easter letter of Athanasius, bishop of Alexandria. Finally, in A.D. 397, the Third Council of Carthage "ratified this canon and placed all other books outside and banned their use in the churches. By the end of the 4th century there was no longer any dispute over the right of any of the 27 books to a place in the canon."[†]

[*] Siegfried H. Horn et al., *Seventh-day Adventist Bible Dictionary* (Washington, D.C.: Review and Herald®, 1960), p. 172.
[†] Ibid., p. 176.

Tuesday
THE BIBLE AS SPECIAL REVELATION

Those who do not believe in God explain the Bible as human beings' attempt to explain the things they see in nature. But Christians believe that the Bible is a record of God's self-disclosure. Paul's statement that "all Scripture is given by inspiration of God," sets the Bible apart from all other books. Read 2 Timothy 3:16, 17.

The Bible is a divine-human document. It "is not a combination of the words of God *and* the words of men. It expresses the word of God *in* the words of men."* The personality of the writer, elements of his culture, and the specific occasion for which he wrote are in evidence in his writing. God did not dictate His words to human secretaries. Yet He spoke His word through these writers.

God used a variety of ways to speak to the writers of the Bible. Some of these ways are described in the Bible itself. What does God say about communicating with prophets? Read Numbers 12:6.

• How does Peter describe the process of inspiration? Read 2 Peter 1:21.

Prophets sometimes had specific experiences of God communicating with them. Read Ezekiel 1:1; Isaiah 6:1, 8, 9; Revelation 1:10. What details of these experiences indicate that they received messages at specific times?

Certainly not all of the books of the Bible came about because of visions and dreams. Some books are simple historical records. How did Luke gather material for the Gospel he wrote? Read Luke 1:1–4.

Regardless of how the Bible writer got the content for his book, by faith we have confidence that God was guiding the process. When Jesus was with His disciples, He taught them directly, face-to-face. What did He tell them about the completeness of their learning? And what promise did He make that gives us insight into how God oversaw the writing of the Scriptures? Read John 16:12, 13; 14:25, 26.

• Disciples' learning?

• Jesus' promise?

Just as Jesus, the Living Word, was divine and human, the Written Word is a divine and human document.

---

* Richard Rice, *Reign of God* (Berrien Springs, Mich.: Andrews University Press, 1985), p. 26; emphasis added.

Wednesday

EVIDENCES OF DIVINE INVOLVEMENT

The human element of the Bible is obvious. Various people across a great span of time made marks on clay or wood or tanned animal hides or **papyri** to record words. The divine element is more elusive. We do not have access to the workings of the Holy Spirit on the minds of the writers. Instead, we have to look for evidences of divine involvement in the completed book itself and its impact on human beings. Three indicators of divine involvement are the Bible's unity of theme, its miraculous preservation over the centuries, and its impact on human beings.

Unity of theme. God is the main Character of the Bible, and His interactions with human beings are chronicled from Genesis through Revelation. In this brief sample of texts from across the Scriptures, trace God's attitude and actions toward His children. Read Genesis 3:15; 12:1–3; Exodus 3:7–10; Isaiah 53:4–6; Luke 2:8–15; John 3:16; 2 Peter 3:9; Revelation 21:1–4. Summarize what these texts say about God's attitude and actions toward human beings.

Miraculous preservation. Based on several dated events in the Old Testament, the first books of the Bible were probably written from about 1446 to 1406 B.C. by Moses during the wandering in the wilderness. How these writings and all the other books of the Bible have been preserved over the millennia would require a book-length explanation. The accuracy of our current copies to the original writings was given strong support in 1947 when the **Dead Sea Scrolls** were found. These texts from as early as the second or third century before Christ have wording that is remarkably similar to the Bibles we hold in our hands today. We can have confidence that our Bibles are faithful to the original writers' messages.

Impact on people. From our own experience and from the experience of others, we have evidence that there is power in the Word of God to change people. What aspects of a person can the Word change? Read Hebrews 4:12.

It is, however, possible to read the Bible without its changing us. Ironically, some highly honored scholars of the Bible do not believe in God. Jesus recognized this possibility even in His day. What did He tell the learned rabbis about their study of Scripture? Read John 5:39.

• How does Paul explain the fact that the Scriptures appear to have no impact on certain people? Read 1 Corinthians 2:13, 14.

KEY TERMS

Papyri—Documents written on "paper" made from the papyrus plant, which grows along the Nile River.
Dead Sea Scrolls—Scrolls discovered between 1947 and 1956 in caves near the Dead Sea; include some of the only known surviving copies of the Old Testament written before 100 B.C.

Thursday
THE ULTIMATE AUTHORITY

The Scriptures give a progressive self-revelation of God. Sometimes the Old Testament prophets who foretold the coming of a Savior did not understand what they were writing, even though they longed to know. Even the angels wondered. How do the writings of the Old Testament prophets and the New Testament apostles (those who preached the Word) work together for our benefit? Read 1 Peter 1:10–12.

God's ultimate self-revelation was given in the Person of Jesus Christ. How does the writer of Hebrews explain the progressive nature of God's self-revelation? What do you consider to be his strongest words declaring Jesus to be the self-revelation of God? Read Hebrews 1:1–3.

Jesus' attitude and use of the Scriptures gave them divine authority. By the time Jesus came to earth, the canon of Scriptures (Old Testament) was definite and well established. What value did Jesus place on the Old Testament Scriptures? Read Matthew 5:17; Luke 24:44; John 10:35.

Jesus affirmed the full authority of the Old Testament Scriptures. When He taught the people, He gave His own words equal authority. In the Sermon on the Mount, what word "formula" did He use to give this status to His own teachings? Read Matthew 5:21, 22, 27, 28, 31, 32.

The most important criterion for selecting books to include in the New Testament was the close relationship of the writer to Jesus or to one of His apostles. Here are all eight or nine New Testament writers and their relationship to Jesus or one of His apostles: Matthew, John, Peter, and Paul were apostles of Jesus. Mark was an associate of both the apostles Peter and Paul. Luke traveled with Paul. The author of Hebrews was either Paul or someone who had contact with him. James and Jude were half brothers of Jesus and associates of the apostles in the early church. So ultimate authority of both the Old and New Testaments rests on the authority of Jesus, the Word who was God. Read John 1:1.

Friday

CHECKING UP

Circle all correct answers.

1. In what ways did Jesus give divine authority to the Old Testament?
   A. He frequently quoted from the books of the Old Testament, using them as authoritative documents.
   B. He told the religious leaders that they made mistakes in their thinking because they did not know the Scriptures.
   C. He explained in detail how God worked with the prophets when they wrote their books.
   D. He used the Old Testament Scriptures to learn about His Father's will and to understand His own mission.

2. In what ways did Jesus give divine authority to the New Testament?
   A. In the Sermon on the Mount, He claimed that His words of interpretation had the same authority as the Old Testament Scriptures.
   B. After His resurrection but before He ascended to heaven, He commissioned certain apostles to record in writing His life and teachings.
   C. He promised that when He was no longer with His disciples, the Holy Spirit would help them remember His words.
   D. The most important standard for admitting a book into the New Testament canon was that the book must have been written by an apostle or a close associate of an apostle.

Examine Your Own Experience

How can you know that the Bible is reliable—that it is trustworthy for you to base your life on its principles? The best test of this is to consider what Scripture says about itself. First, concerning the various claims for truth that we face in life, the Bible says, "To the law and to the testimony! If they do not speak according to this word, it is because there is no light in them" (Isa. 8:20, NKJV). This implies that Scripture is consistent with itself. Second, there is ample evidence of prophetic fulfillment throughout the Bible: "I am God, and there is no other; I am God, and there is none like Me, declaring the end from the beginning" (Isa. 46:9, 10, NKJV). Third, Scripture leads us to the Savior: Jesus "expounded to them in all the Scriptures the things concerning Himself. . . . Then He said to them, 'These are the words which I spoke to you while I was still with you, that all things must be fulfilled which were written in the Law of Moses and the Prophets and the Psalms concerning Me' " (Luke 24:27, 44, NKJV).

More resources on this topic can be found at http://www.InStepWithJesus.org/Journey.

Uncovering the Hidden Past

Archaeology contributes to our understanding of the culture, politics, religions, and daily life of people living during the various periods covered by the Bible. Artifacts from archaeological digs sometimes provide evidence of the reliability of biblical stories, people, and place names. Adventists' interest in the Bible has led them to an interest in archaeology.

Siegfried Horn (1908–1993), archaeologist and Bible scholar, started an archaeological museum (later named for him) at the Seventh-day Adventist Theological Seminary at Andrews University. In 1968, he directed excavations at the site of Tall Hisban. This dig eventually developed into the current Madaba Plains Project, centered at Andrews University's Institute of Archaeology.

A consortium of Adventist colleges and universities sponsor the Madaba Plains Project, which is accredited by the authority of the American Schools of Oriental Research. The Madaba Plains region lies between the Dead Sea and the city of Amman, Jordan—the ancient homeland of the biblical Amorites, Ammonites, and Moabites. Excavations are made in one or more of these major sites each summer, unless prohibited by the political situation: Tall al-'Umayri, Tall Hisban, and Tall Jalul. Adventist universities included in a consortium for the Madaba Plains Project are the following:
- Andrews University, Berrien Springs, Michigan, U.S.A.
- Canadian University College, Lacombe, Alberta, Canada.
- La Sierra University, Riverside, California, U.S.A.

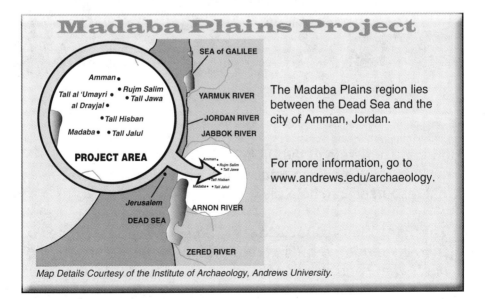

Madaba Plains Project

The Madaba Plains region lies between the Dead Sea and the city of Amman, Jordan.

For more information, go to www.andrews.edu/archaeology.

Map Details Courtesy of the Institute of Archaeology, Andrews University.

HOW TO STUDY THE BIBLE (Part 1)

Key Texts: *Psalm 119:97–104; Isaiah 55:11; Mark 10:17–27; 1 Corinthians 10:1–11; Revelation 22:12, 13*

How can I understand the Bible?
How long does it take to understand what the Bible says?
What resources can help me?

This week's memory text: *" 'So is my word that goes out from my mouth: it will not return to me empty, but will accomplish what I desire and achieve the purpose for which I sent it' "* (Isa. 55:11, NIV).

The Bible is a complex book. In fact, it is a collection of 66 books; 39 are in the Old Testament, and 27 are in the New Testament. These various books span several thousand years and were written to people who lived in cultures that no longer exist.

It takes more than a casual reading to understand the Bible and to receive it as the Word of God for us today. Careful study of the Bible used to be more common among Christians than it is now. People with a secular worldview have no particular interest in reading the Bible, and some Christians seem too busy and distracted to spend the necessary time. Yet, consider what they are missing. In the pages of the Bible, God reveals Himself and His purposes for us. This week we'll begin the task of learning how to study the Bible.

Walking With Jesus in the Real World

A Bible Scholar Gives Safeguards for Study

Dr. Jon Paulien, a New Testament scholar, uses this familiar story in one of his books: a young man who seldom studied his Bible was faced with an important decision and wanted guidance from God. So, after praying, he dropped his Bible on a table, allowing it to open wherever "the Spirit wanted." Without looking, he placed his finger on a text and then read it: "Judas went out and hanged himself." That guidance was depressing and did not seem related to his own decision, so he tried the same method again. This time he read, "Go and do likewise." This humorous story illustrates the danger of interpreting the Bible frivolously. There is certainly a better way.

Early in his life as a Bible scholar, Dr. Paulien realized that people can be unknowingly biased by their own experiences or worldviews to distort what the Bible actually says. To counteract that problem, he made a commitment to pray this prayer before he studied, "I want to know the truth no matter what the cost." God will answer that prayer and the person will pay the cost, Paulien says.

For people who want to learn what the Bible teaches but who are not Bible scholars, Paulien gives the following safeguards for studying Scripture:

1. Pray and be self-distrustful. When you pray for the guidance of the Holy Spirit (as you should), you may gain a sense of self-confidence that your understanding of the text is accurate. Yet your own biases or lack of knowledge may blind you. You also need to pray, "Show me the truth no matter the cost." And that cost may even take you through a painful process of understanding your own deceitful heart.

2. Use a variety of translations. As you see the various ways different translators have tried to express the original Hebrew or Greek meaning in English, you will come to a richer understanding of what the author intended.

3. Spend the majority of your time in the clearest sections of Scripture. "If you spend your time in the trumpets and seals, you will go nuts," Dr. Paulien writes. "Your theology will lose touch with Jesus." The clearer sections of Scripture will give you a theological bedrock.

4. Spend the majority of your time reading the Bible rather than doing word searches in a concordance. With the amazing capabilities of electronic search engines, it is tempting to think that truth can be found in a database. People fail to read entire books of the Bible.

5. Get the critiques of several scholars before coming to a conclusion. Without knowing the original languages and the cultural background of your texts, you may make an obvious error. You should not be discouraged about your challenges of understanding the Bible. Jesus said, " 'If you hold to my teaching, you are really my disciples' " (John 8:31, NIV).

THE MOST IMPORTANT REQUIREMENT

"The most important requirement for effective Bible study is a proper attitude. To learn what God has to say to us in the Bible, we must approach it in the right frame of mind. This includes recognizing the authority of the Bible as the Word of God. We must be willing to submit our preferences and desires to the teachings of the Word. We must be willing to learn, and not just look for ways of reinforcing our preconceptions. We must also seek the guidance of the Holy Spirit. The Bible not only records what God has said in the past; it is also the primary means through which God speaks to us today. We need the assistance of the Spirit in order to discover what he intends for us to hear."*

No other writer in the Bible seemed to treasure the Word of God more than David. Many of his psalms rejoice over the Word. When he wrote the 176-line Psalm 119, he set a real challenge for himself by designing it as an acrostic. The psalm is divided into 22 stanzas, each devoted to a letter of the Hebrew alphabet and each line within that stanza beginning with the same letter. The greatest challenge came, however, when he chose to write about only one topic: his love of the Word. In almost every verse, he uses the word *Word* or one of its synonyms. Read Psalm 119:97–104. Summarize David's attitude toward the Word.

In the entire book of Psalms, David used nine different words to refer to the Word. Read Psalm 119:97–104 again and write all of the words used for "the Word" in this stanza.

Assuming we have the right attitude toward the Bible, there are two distinct tasks involved in studying it, because the Bible is not only a record of what God has said in the past, but it is also the primary means through which He speaks to us today. We need to recognize both of these functions, and we can do that by answering two questions:

1. What did the text mean to the author and the original recipients (what it meant)?
2. What does it mean to us today (what it means)?

Anyone—a believer or not—can find the answer to the first question, but the answer to the second question will come only to the believer who is open to the prompting of the Holy Spirit. The divine inspiration of the Bible is not complete until a person reads it, submits to its instruction, rebuke, or encouragement, and follows what it says.

---

* Richard Rice, *Reign of God* (Berrien Springs, Mich.: Andrews University Press, 1985), p. 39.

THE BIBLE'S BIG PICTURE

If we step back from the Bible and take an overall view of it, we can see that all 66 books are contributing to one story, the story of God and how He relates to human beings. The arrangement of the books in the Bible loosely follows the narrative of this cosmic story, which Adventists have long called "the great controversy."

The first 11 chapters of Genesis reveal the prehistoric events of Creation, the Fall, the Flood, and the Tower of Babel. Beginning with the call of Abraham in Genesis 12, the rest of the Old Testament deals with the history of God's chosen people, the Israelites. In this history, God was preparing a setting for His greatest revelation, the actual, physical embodiment of His Son, Jesus. The individual stories of the Old Testament fit within this overarching drama. What value does Paul still see in these stories for us today? Read 1 Corinthians 10:1–11.

The Old Testament ended as an unfinished story, which is completed in the New Testament. The Gospels give four inspired testimonies on the life and teachings of the incarnated Son of God. The rest of the New Testament reinterprets the Old Testament in the light of the risen Christ, deals with the beginning and spread of Christianity, and gives instructions on how Christians are to live. Revelation, the last book, brings the story of God's plan of salvation to a glorious conclusion. With what majestic words does Christ announce that the entire story of God-and-human history is really about Him? Read Revelation 22:12, 13.

A CLOSER LOOK

Understanding the Bible

Understanding the Bible in deeper ways is an ongoing task of the entire body of Christian believers. Peter said it is not the work of a single individual (2 Pet. 1:19, 20). Yet, each individual must study it for personal benefit.

The range of biblical knowledge is great—from the new Christian who may not even know where to locate books in the Bible to scholars who write commentaries on the Bible. No one person or even generation of people can understand everything in the Bible because it offers an unlimited field for research. Although a few Christians are called to become scholars in order to serve the church, all Christians are called to study the Bible in order to live as disciples.

Wednesday

WHAT DID IT MEAN?
THE CONTEXT

We are going to practice "studying" the Bible. As you probably know, there are different levels of reading and studying the Bible. Without any kind of help, you can read some parts of the Bible and learn much about God's love for human beings, what He has provided for them, and what He expects of them. You can, however, gain much more from your study of the Word if you know how to go about it and have a few basic tools to help you understand. As we learned earlier, the first task of Bible study is to answer the question, What did the text mean to the author and the original recipients? It is for this question that tools for Bible study are most needed. As you use these tools, you must recognize that they are all human products subject to human error.

What tools are needed? Typical tools for Bible study include a good translation of the Bible, a concordance, a Bible dictionary, a Bible handbook, and good commentaries. For information on specific recommendations for these resources, go to www.InStepWithJesus.org.

You may already own some tools. A good Bible will have subheadings, Jesus' words printed in red, poetry printed in poetic form, footnotes, a cross-referencing system, and maybe maps and a brief concordance at the back. To learn how to use the footnotes and cross-referencing, you need to read the preface or introduction of your Bible.

The passage we will "practice on" is Mark 10:17–27, the story of the "rich young ruler."

To answer the question, What did it mean to the author and the original recipients? we need to consider both the *context* and the *content* of the passage. First read the text.

Questions of context. In a limited sense, *context* refers to the verses surrounding the passage. But primarily, questions of context fall into two categories: historical and literary. To answer them typically requires resources in addition to the Bible itself.

Historical context refers to the time the event occurred and/or the time the author wrote his message. It can include the political, religious, and social climate as well as the occasion and the purpose that motivated the writer to write. (Mark is especially interested in explaining the nature of Jesus' Messiahship as the Suffering Servant. It is believed that what he wrote he learned primarily from Peter.)

Literary context refers to the literary type to which the book belongs. (The book of Mark is a Gospel, which is a unique kind of book that relates the life and teachings of Jesus.)

Thursday
WHAT DID IT MEAN?
THE CONTENT

Once you know the historical and literary context of the passage you are studying, you are ready to turn to the content itself.

Questions of content. As obvious as it seems, we must emphasize the importance of reading Bible passages carefully and thoughtfully. Read Mark 10:17–27 twice. We will ask a few key questions raised by the story. If you are familiar with the New Testament, you may be able to answer the questions yourself. Because some questions can be answered only by consulting other sources, brief answers have been given in parentheses. If you have resources available, compare these explanations to the explanations given in your resources.

• Mark identifies the man who came to Jesus only as "a man." Why is this man called "the rich young ruler"? (In a parallel passage, Luke identifies the man as "a certain ruler." Editors add "rich" to the subheading because the man had "great wealth"; they probably add "young" because the man refers to his boyhood.)

• What would the young ruler and other Jews have understood about Jesus' comment that "only God is good"? (Because Jews believed that only God is good, they might have considered the possibility that Jesus was claiming to be God.)

• When Jesus quoted the last six commandments, why did He change "do not covet" to "do not defraud"? (Defrauding is an example of coveting, and it is a special temptation of the wealthy.)

• Why were the disciples amazed when Jesus said that it is hard for people with riches to enter the kingdom of God? (Jews considered wealth to be a blessing of God, given because of a person's piety.)

• When Jesus said " 'it is easier for a camel to go through the eye of a needle than for a rich man to enter the kingdom of God,' " what was He referring to? (At the time this story was written, there was no gate in Jerusalem named "Eye of the Needle." Jesus was simply using exaggeration to dramatically make a point.)

Now read Mark 10:17–27 again.

Our study of this passage will continue next week to answer the question, What does it mean to us today?

Friday

CHECKING UP

Place the letter of the term in the blank beside the words that describe it. (Note: There is one more term than description.)

Description		Term
1. ___	First task of Bible study	A. **Literary genre**
2. ___	Second task of Bible study	B. Great controversy
3. ___	Law, prophets, writings, Gospels, epistles	C. What it means
4. ___	Text references listed in the middle column of most Bibles and keyed to texts on that page	D. Proper attitude
5. ___	Twenty-seven books	E. Historical context
6. ___	The big picture or the overarching story of the Bible	F. Concordance
7. ___	Most important requirement for effective Bible study	G. Old Testament
8. ___	Thirty-nine books	H. New Testament
9. ___	Examples: poetry, narrative, history, letters	I. What it meant
10. ___	Time and culture when Bible writers wrote	J. Cross-referencing
		K. Sections of the Bible

Examine Your Own Experience

Place an **X** on the line to indicate where you are now in your Bible knowledge. Place an ★ on the line to indicate where you want to be in five years.

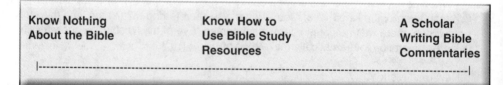

Know Nothing About the Bible	Know How to Use Bible Study Resources	A Scholar Writing Bible Commentaries
|--|		

Extend Your Learning

If your Bible has cross-referencing, read the preface and/or the introduction of the Bible to find out the meaning of the symbols used. If your Bible does not have cross-referencing, buy a Bible that does have it. Your pastor or group leader may be able to help you acquire such a Bible if it is not financially possible for you to buy one.

More resources on this topic can be found at http://www.InStepWithJesus.org/Journey.

KEY TERMS

Literary genre—A category of writing based on style, form, and content.

Which Bible Version Should I Use?

With so many English versions of the Bible available, people get confused over which is best or most accurate. To make a decision on a version to purchase, you need to know the philosophy that guided the translators.

Translators must make a decision whether they will try to translate word for word or thought for thought or write a paraphrase. If they translate word for word, the sentences are very accurate to the original, but may have awkward word order, unpleasant rhythm, or strange meanings when idioms are used in the original. If they translate thought by thought, the English sounds pleasant and the sentences are easy to understand, but important meanings from original words may be lost and the translator has more freedom to suggest what he thinks the text means. If a translator writes a paraphrase (most are written by single individuals), he or she first interprets what the original means to the best of their ability and within their own theological understanding and then puts the words into common, everyday English that sounds like any contemporary book.

Your purpose helps to determine which translation is best for you. Think of the different versions as being located along a continuum from closest to the original (word for word) to furthest from the original (paraphrase). If you want to study your Bible in careful detail, you will select a Bible located at or near the word for word end of the continuum. If you want a Bible to study and yet to be easier to understand and to sound good when read in public, you will select a version located in the center or thought for thought category. If you want to get a general idea of what the Bible says and if you understand that the translator's theology is embedded in the wording, you can select a paraphrase.

By comparing several versions of the Bible on the same text, you will gain subtle differences in meaning as various translators do their best to translate into English the thought the original writer intended. Remember that every translation is to a greater or lesser extent an interpretation and that paraphrased Bibles are actually Bible commentaries.

To become a real Bible scholar, you will need to learn Hebrew and Greek, and then you can use an interlinear Bible, which prints the Hebrew or Greek words with their English equivalents underneath each word.

This chart locates some popular Bible versions on the continuum of word for word to paraphrase. The Bible lessons in this Sabbath School Bible study guide use the New King James Version, unless otherwise specified.

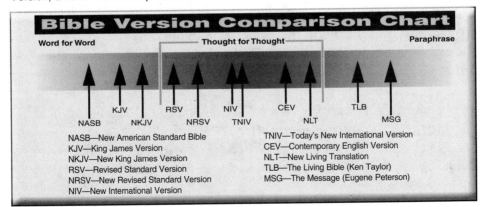

Bible Version Comparison Chart

Word for Word   Thought for Thought   Paraphrase

KJV   RSV   NIV   CEV   TLB
NASB   NKJV   NRSV   TNIV   NLT   MSG

NASB—New American Standard Bible
KJV—King James Version
NKJV—New King James Version
RSV—Revised Standard Version
NRSV—New Revised Standard Version
NIV—New International Version

TNIV—Today's New International Version
CEV—Contemporary English Version
NLT—New Living Translation
TLB—The Living Bible (Ken Taylor)
MSG—The Message (Eugene Peterson)

HOW TO STUDY THE BIBLE (Part 2)

Key Texts: *Deuteronomy 6:4–9; Matthew 12:43–45; 17:5; Mark 10:17–27; Romans 12:2; 2 Corinthians 10:4, 5; Philippians 2:5; 4:8; Hebrews 4:12; Revelation 3:20*

What can I do to make the Bible relevant to my own life?
Are reading and studying the only tools available?
Should reading or studying my Bible always give me understanding and joy?

This week's memory text: *"The word of God is living and powerful, and sharper than any two-edged sword, piercing even to the division of soul and spirit, and of joints and marrow, and is a discerner of the thoughts and intents of the heart"* (Heb. 4:12, NKJV).

Once you know the basic principles for learning what a Bible passage meant to the original author and the original recipients, you are ready to learn what the passage means for you today. The first type of learning is "head knowledge"; the second is "heart knowledge." The "two-edged sword" can pierce your self-deceptive armor at any point of your study.

Both kinds of study are essential as Jesus demonstrated with the disciples on the road to Emmaus. Those disciples recalled their emotion during Jesus' teaching: " 'Were not our hearts burning within us while he . . . opened the Scriptures to us?' " (Luke 24:32, NIV). This is the emotional response you will have as Jesus speaks to you through the Scriptures, and you learn what they mean to you personally.

Walking With Jesus in the Real World

The Stripping Process—Fredrick Russell

*New believers are not the only ones who go through the "denying self process" to follow Jesus. Pastors, too, must "lose their life to gain it."**

Prior to the call we had not even heard of the church. We had accepted it sight unseen.

Baltimore is a city of row houses. In many areas of the city today, young urban professionals are moving in and snatching up row houses, but the section of the city where the church is located didn't have to worry about this.

The church was a two-story red brick structure with a cornerstone proudly announcing 1866. The Miracle Temple congregation had occupied it for a little more than 20 years.

We were greeted warmly by three deacons. While their warmth touched me, I was overwhelmed by my initial reaction to the place. It was relatively clean, but one definitely felt its age. Attempts had been made to improve things, but it still felt dark and dingy.

My "ministerial pride" had not just taken a hit on my first day at Miracle Temple, it was under assault. All around me were the clear, unmistakable signs that I was in a "go nowhere" situation, in a bad part of the city, with a small congregation, in a building that had seen better days.

Three weeks after my first Sabbath at Miracle Temple, I stood at the window on the second floor of the church-owned row house where my church office was located. Rat droppings were on my desk, the yellowed-stained walls were bare, and the room was cold. I actually sensed God speaking to me about the selfishness of my attitude, my quest to be always on top, the problem of my pride, and my proverbial lack of dependence on Him. In that brief moment, I saw some of the "darkness" inside my own heart, and I didn't like what God was showing me.

I made a request of God that would change my life, when I prayed this simple prayer: "God, please give me a vision for Miracle Temple, and I will give it all I've got." A peace and calm suddenly came over me.

The eight years since that time have been a whirlwind. God has been teaching me daily, nurturing me in my dependence on Him, and convincing me of the value of rising early in the morning to seek His face. Prayer is a nonnegotiable for me. I have a deepening desire to be more and more with God as He has always wanted to be with me. We're finally on the same page. Yes, of course, I still struggle at moments with the "stuff" of the heart, but I'm more aware of it and confess it immediately when it rises in my spirit. I watched God do the "stripping" process in my life, having to take me down in order to build me up again His way. I fought God, and thankfully, I lost.

---

* Fredrick Russell, "The Stripping Process," *Ministry*®, September 2004, www.MinistryMagazine.org. Used by permission.

Monday

HEARING THE WORD

When the risen and glorified Christ appeared to John in vision on the **Isle of Patmos**, He gave messages to the seven churches. In His message to the seventh church, the church at **Laodicea**, Christ included this promise: " 'Behold, I stand at the door and knock. If anyone hears My voice and opens the door, I will come in to him and dine with him, and he with Me' " (Rev. 3:20, NKJV).

Here we see Christ taking the initiative to interact with us, to dine with us. Dining is an appropriate metaphor for the second task of Bible study—finding out what the text or passage means to us today. Read the promise again. What two things are we to do to respond to Christ's dining invitation?

1.

2.

Spend some time thinking about what these actions would look like in your own life.

In both Hebrew (the language of the Old Testament) and Greek (the language of the New Testament), the word *hear* has a rich meaning that includes the concept of "listen" and "pay attention to," which results in doing what you hear.

The word *hear* is the first word in the Shema, the great Jewish confession of faith first spoken by Moses as he prepared the people to enter the Promised Land. Read the Shema in Deuteronomy 6:4–9. How are the people supposed to treat the words given through the prophet?

At another significant point in salvation history, God Himself spoke. What was the occasion and what did God want the disciples to do? Read the verses before and after Matthew 17:5.

Both the "dining" and "hearing" actions involve relationship. Christ invites us to dine with Him, and God the Father tells us to hear what Christ has to say. When we enter into this relationship and listen to the words of and about Christ, we are deeply affected. What was the reaction of people who listened to Jesus in each situation below?

• Mark 1:22 (the people)

• John 7:45–47 (officers of Jesus' "enemies")

• Luke 24:27, 32 (His own disciples)

As you open your heart and listen to the Word, which is the second task of Bible study, you will be entering into a relationship with Jesus. That's what Revelation 3:20 says.

KEY TERMS

Isle of Patmos—A small Greek island in the Aegean Sea, where John was banished by Emperor Domitian.
Laodicea—The seventh and last church in the book of Revelation; known for its lukewarmness.

Tuesday

SEEKING TRANSFORMATION

God desires human beings "to be conformed to the image of His Son" (Rom. 8:29, NKJV). Because human beings are sinners, this process does not come naturally; we must be transformed by the power of God. At the Creation, God spoke human beings into existence. In our re-creation, God again uses His Word. Read the following texts and explain what they tell you about the process of transformation into the image of Christ: Romans 12:2; 2 Corinthians 10:4, 5; Philippians 2:5; 4:8.

• Where does transformation occur?
• What model do we have?
• On what should our thoughts dwell?

When you became a follower of Jesus, you probably began to see certain things in your life that really don't belong in a Christian's life—maybe such things as cheating, envy, abusive behavior, or addictive habits. If these things are not replaced with good things and good habits, what will be the result? Jesus told a parable to answer this very question. Read Matthew 12:43–45. What will happen?

It is frightening to know that true transformation into Christlikeness is humanly impossible. The amazing thing to know is that with God's grace "all things are possible."
We open ourselves to the grace of God as we take up the second task of reading and studying His Word. Here are the steps for finding out what the Word means to us:
1. Read the text thoughtfully.
2. Meditate on the text.
3. Pray in response to the text.
4. Choose a phrase or idea to take with you for worship and obedience.
In the lesson segments for the next two days, you will practice this type of study.

A CLOSER LOOK

Imagination
Some people are afraid of the word *imagination*. Others see imagination as a great gift or tool of creativity and understanding. Why this difference? In part, the confusion comes over the words *imagination* and *imaginary*. *Imaginary* means "lacking factual reality." *Imagination* means "creative ability to enter into a situation or to form something not known before." Using the imagination in Bible study means to place yourself in the context of the passage.
Notice how Ellen White encourages readers of the Sermon on the Mount: "Let us in imagination go back to that scene, and, as we sit with the disciples on the mountainside, enter into the thoughts and feelings that filled their hearts. Understanding what the words of Jesus meant to those who heard them, we may discern in them a new vividness and beauty, and may also gather for ourselves their deeper lessons."*

---
* *Thoughts From the Mount of Blessing*, p. 1.

Wednesday

READ CAREFULLY

Last week we learned that Bible study involves two tasks. Find out (1) what it meant to the original writers and recipients, and (2) what it means to us today. Using Mark 10:17–27, we practiced the first task. Today and tomorrow we will again use the same passage to practice the second task.

Step 1: Read the text thoughtfully. Pray for the Holy Spirit to guide your understanding; then read the passage twice. Since this passage is a narrative, you may be able to "enter the story" if you imagine yourself as a bystander or as a movie director who wants to film the scene. Then ask specific questions about the passage. Read Mark 10:17–27. Here are some questions as examples.

• What did the young ruler want?

• What kind of person do you think the neighbors thought the young man was?

• What emotions are shown in this passage

  ◦ by Jesus? (Read verse 21.)

  ◦ by the rich young ruler? (Read verse 22.)

  ◦ by the disciples? (Read verses 24, 26.)

Do you think the young man felt that something might be keeping him from what he wanted? Or do you think he just wanted Jesus to compliment him on what "a fine young man" he was?

Jesus told the rich young man that he lacked one thing. Jesus didn't say what he lacked, He just told him what to do about it. What three things did Jesus tell him to do?
  1.

  2.

  3.

• So, what do you think he lacked?

What is the relationship between Jesus' answer to the young man in verse 19 and His answer to His disciples in verse 27? The questions are the same.

Does Jesus expect all disciples to sell all they have, give the money to the poor, and follow Him?

Is Jesus advocating a life of poverty or a life of discipleship or some other way of life?

MEDITATE ON THE TEXT

After you have thoughtfully read the Bible passage and asked questions to see all the details, you are now ready for the next step, which is meditation. When the word *meditation* is mentioned, some Christians become quite concerned because in our culture it too often brings to mind the Eastern form of meditation in which a person attempts to empty his or her mind in order "to become one with the cosmos."

Christian meditation is far from that model. Christian meditation is filling the mind with thoughtful reflection on the Word. "Meditation engages us at the level of the 'heart' in its biblical sense, where memory, experience, thoughts, feelings, hopes, desires, intuitions, and intentions are joined."*

Step 2: Meditate on the text. Reading and meditating are separate functions, but not necessarily done at separate times. You will probably move back and forth through reading and meditating. Throughout this entire process, your overall thought should be, *What does God want to say to me through this text?*

Read again Mark 10:17–27 and then reflect on these questions, which are given as examples of questions that are appropriate for meditation.

• Is something more important to me than salvation?

• If so, what might Jesus ask me to do to set my priorities straight?

• What can I learn about Jesus in this passage?

• Do I realize in a personal way that earning salvation by keeping the commandments is impossible?

• Do I know of friends or relatives who have accepted Jesus' invitation to follow Him and any who have rejected His invitation? What are their lives like now?

ADVENTESE

Food Terms
- **Haystacks:** Popular with young people, this casual dish usually consists of corn chips, beans, salsa, onions, lettuce, tomatoes, and grated cheese, all piled up on a plate.
- **Health foods:** Refers to commercial products made to imitate various kinds of meat; does not refer to the quality of nutrition.
- **Special K® loaf or cottage cheese loaf:** Probably the most well-known Adventist vegetarian entrée; made of Special K® cereal, cottage cheese, eggs, and seasonings.
- **Vegetarian:** One who eats *only* vegetables, fruits, nuts, grains, eggs, and dairy products.
- **Vegan:** One who eats *only* vegetables, fruits, nuts, and grains.

* Marjorie Thompson, *Soul Feast: An Invitation to the Christian Spiritual Life* (Louisville, Ky.: Westminster Knox Press, 1995), p. 23.

CHECKING UP

Respond to the Text

While you are reading and meditating on the Bible passage, you may find that the Holy Spirit uses the Word as a "two-edged sword" to truly cut to your heart and show you parts of yourself that you had not been aware of before. Or you may get an insight into who Jesus is and what He has done and is doing for you. This new knowledge calls for a response from you. And that first response will be prayer.

Step 3: Pray in response to the text. We will continue studying the passage about the rich young ruler. Read again Mark 10:17–27. Even though Jesus knew the young ruler would choose not to follow Him, He looked at him and "loved him."

Does this tell you something about Jesus? Do you feel like praising Him because of His great love for sinners? Then, in prayer, praise Him. Do you feel impressed that something in your life is more important to you right now than following Jesus? If so, do you want to set your priorities straight? Or do you at least want to be made willing to set them straight? Pray to God that He will provide the necessary motivation and strength. This is the first step in obeying the Word.

Step 4: Choose a phrase or idea to take with you for worship and obedience. After you have completed your study to uncover what the text means to you, you will want to choose a phrase or an idea to put in your memory and to live it through worship and obedience. Here are some suggestions for the passage you have been studying:

- Only God is good.
- Jesus looked at him and loved him.
- How hard it is for those who trust in riches to enter the kingdom of God.
- With God, all things are possible.

This entire process of studying, meditating on, and responding in prayer to the Word brings you into a relationship with Jesus, the Living Word.

Examine Your Own Experience

Has the method of Bible study that you have been doing the past two weeks been a new experience for you? Do you see its value? Discuss these questions with your study group.

More resources on this topic can be found at http://www.InStepWithJesus.org/Journey.

Bible Study to Change Your Life

For the past two weeks, we have been learning how to study the Bible. We have said that there are two parts or two tasks to this process. To provide a handy reference sheet, we will summarize both tasks on this one page.

Task One
What did the text mean to the author and the original recipients?

Always begin your study of the Bible with prayer for the guidance of the Holy Spirit.
• Carefully read the text or passage at least two times.
• Consider matters of context.
  ○ In what literary form was the passage written (parable, history, poem, etc.)?
  ○ What is the meaning of the texts surrounding the passage you are studying?
  ○ By whom and to whom was this written?
  ○ What was the author's purpose?
• Consider the content.
  ○ Read carefully every phrase and word, asking yourself, "How would the original hearers have understood this?" You will probably have to consult some resources.
  ○ What do you learn about Jesus?

Task Two
What does the text mean to us today?

Continue your study with a prayer that the Holy Spirit will help you "hear" what God wants to tell you through this passage.
• Read the text carefully through the lens of what it might mean to you.
  ○ If a story, place yourself in the setting to "listen and see" the action.
• Meditate on the text.
  ○ Ponder each word and phrase.
  ○ Compare its teaching with your own life. What message does God have for you? What does Jesus invite you to know or to do?
• Pray in response to the text, whether confession, repentance, praise, strength, etc.
• Take a phrase or idea with you to remember throughout the day.

LESSON 13

MAKING TIME FOR GOD

Key Texts: *Matthew 26:36–40; Mark 10:23–27; Luke 6:12, 13; John 3:3; 7:16, 17; 12:49, 50; 15:5–10; 17:15–19; 1 Corinthians 15:31*

How can I keep from being influenced by my secular culture to doubt God?

How much time does it take to get to know Jesus?

What elements help create Spirit-filled devotions?

This week's memory text: " *'I am the vine, you are the branches. He who abides in Me, and I in him, bears much fruit; for without Me you can do nothing' "* (John 15:5, NKJV).

Sunday

We need to make time for God because we live in hostile, enemy territory where God is denied, ignored, or blasphemed. As sociologists point out, no one is immune from the influence of his or her own culture. Not so many years ago, our homes served as little fortresses that could shut out the media, which today are the chief purveyors of culture. But no longer. Television and the Internet deliver information of all kinds not just to our doorstep but into the intimate, unguarded spaces of our homes. Only by making and keeping a determined commitment to commune with God through His Word and through prayer can we, by His grace, reject the lives admired in the culture and live the lives He is re-creating us to live.

Walking With Jesus in the Real World

Loving the Right Thing—*Eugene Matthews**

I grew up in an Adventist home. My father was an elder. I was baptized at the age of 14. I even read my Bible through as part of the Pathfinder program. But I was not really a part of the church nor was I following God as I should. I have been living a life of sin.

Eventually, as a financial and accounting consultant, I worked for various government agencies. Then I got a high-paying job with a financial firm as a senior financial analyst. After work my coworkers and I would go to bars and I would "nurse a beer" for an evening.

One Friday evening, I was driving home in my prized BMW when a truck suddenly stopped in front of me. I rear-ended it and totaled my car. I wasn't hurt badly, so I took it in stride. But then, a couple of weeks later, I got laid off.

Around March my brother told me of a TV channel sponsored by Adventists. I never thought that anything religious on TV could hold my attention. But I got hooked on Hope TV.

Things weren't going very well with my wife and me. This is my third marriage. One morning we were arguing, and I told her that I didn't think our marriage was going to work out.

"Have you ever loved anyone in your life?" she asked.

I didn't say anything, but I started looking back at my life. I had never loved anyone except myself. I went downstairs, got on my knees, and asked God to help me.

On Sabbath I went to church. From that time on, I have been going every Sabbath. My life has changed. I will soon be re-baptized.

I have converted our theater room into my meditation room. As part of my cleansing process, I got rid of more than 600 videos, keeping the G-rated ones. Every day I have worship by myself, morning and evening. My wife isn't interested but I uphold her and my two stepdaughters before God every morning and evening.

For morning worship, I pray briefly then read several chapters in the Bible. I'm also reading *Steps to Christ* (for the second time), *The Desire of Ages,* and *Christ's Object Lessons.* Then I pour my heart out to God. Because I am not working, my time with God can last over an hour.

I started keeping a daily journal after it was suggested to me in a book I was reading. It's a prayer journal, keeping track of the things I've asked God for and the results. I call it "My Spiritual Journey," and it has made me reflect on what I am doing during the day. Sometimes I will start to say something unkind, and I'll stop. The Holy Spirit helps me to monitor myself in my thoughts, speech, and actions. So each morning, I pray, "Today I want to be like Jesus." It's amazing what God can do for us if we are willing to let Him. This life is new to me, but it has lifted me up. I never used to pay any attention to what I said or did.

I'm still looking for a job and our house is in danger of being foreclosed. I pray, "Father, whatever will happen, will happen. I'm just glad that You're with me." I believe that I've been so broken spiritually that it's taking time to put me back together. Whatever happens, I'm at peace.

* A pseudonym.

Monday

SECULAR DRIFT

If you are a new Christian or a new member of the Seventh-day Adventist Church, you may look around at the people in the church you attend and wonder, *Shouldn't people who have been Christians a long time be more and more joyful about Jesus? Shouldn't they be more and more enthusiastic about telling others of what He has done and is doing for them?*

For some that is true. Yet, strangely, for others it seems they are less and less enthusiastic. A major reason is what Jon Paulien in his book, *Present Truth in the Real World,* calls "secular drift." No Christian sets out to become secular. But because the culture is like a great river of secularism and every person is in a little boat on that river, we just drift along with the current unless we take action against it.

Some Christians try to get out of this river. That is, they try to escape from their culture and live in a safe fortress of their own making. What does Jesus have to say about this matter? In His great prayer on the night of His arrest, while He was still with His disciples, He prayed especially for them. Read John 17:15–19. What complex relationship does Jesus want His disciples to have with the world around them?

• In addition to Jesus' request that His Father protect the disciples, what does He say will "sanctify" them?

From his years of observation as an Adventist pastor and seminary professor, Paulien describes the process of secular drift in terms of steps. Although the steps may differ with individual people, they can be instructive for all of us.

1. Private prayer is the first to go.

2. Bible study is next affected. Even though Bible study may continue, it tends to have less and less personal significance.

3. Personal standards of behavior begin to erode. This may be the first public indication of secular drift.

4. Church attendance becomes irregular until it finally becomes more trouble than it is worth.

5. Influences in society cause a person to doubt the Bible, to doubt the afterlife, and to doubt whether there really is a God.*

So, what are the safeguards against secular drift?

---

* Jon Paulien, *Present Truth in the Real World: The Adventist's Struggle to Keep and Share Faith in a Secular Society* (Nampa, Idaho: Pacific Press® Publishing Association, 1993), pp. 62–65.

Tuesday

HOW JESUS MADE TIME FOR GOD

As "the Word [that] became flesh and dwelt among us" (John 1:14, NKJV), Jesus entered hostile territory when He took on human form to live in the world among sinners. Before this incarnation, He had face-to-face communion with God the Father. As a human being, His communion with God the Father took the forms that are available to all of us. His close communion with His Father gave Him understanding of the Father's will and the power to do it.

Communing with the Father through prayer. One of the first things we learn about Jesus is that prayer was important to Him. Read these texts and meditate on what they tell us about Jesus' prayer life: Mark 1:35; Luke 5:15, 16; 6:12. What time of day did Jesus typically pray?

• Describe the places where He prayed.

• When Jesus was facing important decisions or challenges, how long did He pray? Read Matthew 26:36–40; Luke 6:12, 13.

Communing with the Father through Scripture. Most of what we know about Jesus' study of Scripture is by inference; that is, we know He studied the Word because He quoted it frequently. Even by age 12, He knew a great deal about Scripture. On one occasion in the synagogue, He read from the Isaiah scroll (Luke 4:16–19). According to Jesus, what is the source of His teachings (doctrines, words)? Read John 7:16, 17; 12:49, 50.

Communing with the Father through obedience. Educators know that the most powerful type of learning is experiential learning. We learn by doing. We develop relationships with other people by working with them. Jesus' relationship with the Father was so close that He described it as "abiding in Him" (remaining in Him). What created this closeness? Read John 15:9, 10.

Knowing and doing are intimately linked. The reward is a close relationship with God.

Wednesday

BASICS OF DAILY DEVOTIONS

> As the deer pants for the water brooks,
> So pants my soul for You, O God.
> My soul thirsts for God, for the living God.
> (Ps. 42:1, 2, NKJV).

In these poetic words of the psalmist, we learn the first essential for daily devotions: a longing for God. We come into His presence with a sense of worship. In addition to a spirit of worship, most Christians would agree that other essential elements for daily devotions are prayer and study of the Bible, which includes meditation.

Bible reading/study and meditation. If you were to do a survey of people who regularly have daily devotions and ask them, "How do you choose what you will read?" you would find a variety of answers. Some will use a daily devotional book, some will read chapter by chapter through a Bible book, some will decide what they need to read at the beginning of their devotions. Others may focus on a topic; a few will take on the challenge of reading the Bible through in a year. But careful Bible study takes time and must be limited to small portions of Scripture.

Getting up in the morning and deciding, *Today I need to get [whatever you feel you need at the moment] from the Bible,* may be helpful at specific times, but it is not a solid plan for consistent Bible reading.

You need to have a plan in mind. If you just choose to read what you already know, you will limit what God can say to you. If you are consistent with a planned reading of the Bible, you will discover that the Holy Spirit will often use the words for that day to give you a word from the Lord that amazingly speaks to your need.

Prayer. As you hear God speaking to you through your reading and meditation on Scripture, you will be drawn to respond to Him. You do that through prayer: (1) praising Him for His goodness, His offer of forgiveness and eternal life, and His great love for you; (2) confessing your sins; and (3) asking Him for strength to do His will and for His blessings on yourself, others, and His work in the world. It is through this two-way communication of His Word and your prayer that you will recognize the presence of God.

OTHER MATTERS TO CONSIDER

When Jesus taught the disciples, He often used illustrations from nature. To describe the close relationship that He wants with each of us, He used that beautiful symbol of the grapevine and its branches. Read John 15:5–8. What is the result of your abiding ("remaining," NIV) in Jesus?

• What happens if you don't abide in Him?

• In verse 7 Jesus shows a close relationship between your abiding in Him and your abiding in what else?

Here you find motivation for making your devotional time a priority in your life.

Time. What do people identify as the number one obstacle to their having consistent devotions or time with God? "No time." This old cliché is usually right: where there's a will, there's a way. If you are a beginner, it is more important to be consistent than to spend a large amount of time. Choose a realistic amount of time and seriously commit to it. As you build the habit of making time for God, it is good to have a set time rather than to have a set amount that you want to read because you also want to have time for meditation and prayer.

Frequency. There are at least three clues as to the frequency that Jesus made time for communing with the Father: His frequent praying, His frequent quoting of Scripture, and His frequent reference to doing His Father's will. Luke actually reports on the frequency of times that Jesus spent in solitude and in prayer. Read Luke 5:15, 16. What does Luke report as the frequency?

Secularism says, "The kingdom of the self is all there is. Go for it." Jesus urges us to enter the "kingdom of God." The Greek word for "kingdom" can be more meaningfully translated into English as "reign." So what we see is that the reign of self is in opposition to the reign of God. What does Paul say he must do to overcome the reign of self and how frequently? Read 1 Corinthians 15:31.

• What does Jesus say it takes to enter the kingdom of God? Read John 3:3.

To have the abundant life that Jesus promises, it takes a daily commitment to reject the reign of self (die daily) and submit to the reign of God (be born again). Fulfilling this commitment is actually an impossible task for us on our own, but what promise did Jesus give us? Read Mark 10:23–27.

Friday

CHECKING UP

More Matters to Consider

Place. It is best to have your devotions in the same location each day. That location could be a room, a corner of a room, a desk, or simply a certain chair. Pastor Dwight Nelson once explained to a group of seminarians why consistency of place is important. He said that the smallest change in scenery causes a distraction. "I sit so that I cannot see out the window because even the seasonal changes are distracting," he said.

Solitude. Family worship and small-group study are important, but they should not take the place of your own private, daily time in God's presence. In your home you may not be able to find solitude unless everyone else is asleep or has left the house for the day. What do these texts tell us about the setting that Jesus chose for praying: Mark 1:35; Luke 5:16?

Commitment and patience. Perhaps more people would be consistent in daily devotions if every day they had a dramatic experience of the presence of God. That doesn't always happen. God sometimes seems to be far from us. Read Psalm 22:1, 2. Do you know who in the New Testament quoted the words of this psalm?

A seminary professor says, "There are still passages I sit before again and again and again, awaiting the Word, and as yet, it has not come. . . . But the secret is to keep coming back to those passages to sit before them in receptivity, and to listen. Even when we don't hear anything, just the act of adopting that posture is spiritually forming."*

Devotional books. Many Spirit-filled devotional books (including exceptional daily devotional books) can teach you about God's ways. *Steps to Christ, The Desire of Ages,* and *Thoughts From the Mount of Blessing* are excellent Ellen White books to begin with. You can judge whether a book is a good devotional book by whether it leads you to read the Bible for yourself.

Journaling. Journaling is simply keeping a written record of your thoughts that you have during your devotional time. There are a variety of things that you can record: insights from texts, messages that you feel God has for you, prayers to God, and answers to prayers.

More resources on this topic can be found at http://www.InStepWithJesus.org/Journey.

---

* Robert M. Mulholland, *Shaped by the Word* (Nashville, Tenn.: Upper Room, 1985), p. 115.

Examples of Daily Devotional Plans

Choose your best time of day for your devotions. Because of your schedule, you may have to divide your devotions into different times within the day.

15-minute Devotional Plan
- Pray for guidance of the Holy Spirit.
- Study the Sabbath School lesson.
- Pray.

30-minute Devotional Plan A
- Pray for guidance of the Holy Spirit.
- Read passage in the Bible, making your way slowly through one Gospel.
- Study the Sabbath School lesson.
- Pray.

30-minute Devotional Plan B*
- Prayer for guidance of the Holy Spirit.
- Sing a praise song.
- Read passage in the Bible, making your way slowly through one book of New Testament.
- Keep a journal of key learnings and questions.
- Pray.

60-minute Devotional Plan A*
- Read/say from memory Revelation 3:20.
- Pray for guidance of the Holy Spirit.
- Read/pray a psalm each day.
- Study a passage using the two-tasks method; use resources when appropriate.
- Keep a journal of key learnings and questions.
- Pray, especially intercessory prayer.

60-minute Devotional Plan B*
- Pray for guidance of the Holy Spirit.
- Follow a two-year Bible reading plan, reading in both the Old Testament and New Testament.
- Pray, especially intercessory prayer.
- Keep a prayer journal.
- Read in a devotional book. (When the SS lesson is not studied during devotional time, choose a different time of day to study it.)
- Praise through prayer or song.*

Make Your Learning Real

Now it is time for you to put into practice what you have learned this week about devotions. Design a plan for your daily devotions. Share it with your study group or at least one other person. Have the group or your friend hold you accountable for actually putting the plan into practice.

---

* Robert M. Mulholland, *Shaped by the Word* (Nashville, Tenn.: Upper Room, 1985), p. 115.

Notes

Notes

Notes

Notes

Notes